Behind Painted Walls

Florence C. Lister

Behind Painted Walls

Incidents in Southwestern Archaeology

University of New Mexico Press
Albuquerque

frontispiece: Contemporary interpretation of a Kuaua mural figure. Paul Goodbear, 1936, Robert H. Lister collection.

© 2000 University of New Mexico Press
All rights reserved.
First edition

Library of Congress Cataloging-in-Publication Data

Lister, Florence Cline.
    Behind painted walls : incidents in Southwestern
archaeology / Florence C. Lister. — 1st ed.
        p.   cm.
    Includes bibliographical references and index.
        ISBN 0-8263-2189-5 (cloth) —
        ISBN 0-8263-2190-9 (pbk.)
        1. Pueblo Indians—Antiquities.   2. Mural
painting and decoration—Southwest, New.
    3. Archaeology—Southwest, New—History.
    4. Southwest, New—Antiquities.   I. Title.
        E99.P9   L49 2000
        979'.01—dc21
                                        00-008078

Contents

Figures and Map

Behind Painted Walls

The Reasons Why

The pursuit of archaeology has two sides: one serious and one not-so-serious. This book aims to give armchair enthusiasts some of the flavor of both.

Five northern Southwestern sites have been selected for discussion because they yielded the most extensive provocative wall paintings thus far discovered among the remains of the prehistoric Pueblo peoples who inhabited the Colorado Plateau. Further, each of the five ruins considered had its own unique place both in the area's prehistory and in the evolving discipline of Southwestern archaeology. The paintings at Lowry Ruin out on the western flanks of the Pueblo world set the stage for what was to come. Those at Gran Quivira (Las Humanas) reveal a late provincialism on the eastern frontier. The three communities in between — Kuaua, Awatovi-Kawaika-a, and Pottery Mound — exhibited the apex developments in polychromatic ritualistic imagery.

Prior to work at these ruins, explorers and excavators had noted a few painted images on interior walls of ancestral Pueblo dwellings. Most notable were those in Cliff Palace on the Mesa Verde in southwestern

Sites in text having kiva mural paintings. Map drawn by Claire Lister.

Colorado, in Aztec Ruins in northwestern New Mexico, and in Mummy Cave in Canyon del Muerto, northeastern Arizona. They all were monochromatic, simple in style and extent, and of the same cultural phase as Lowry Ruin. Of those mentioned above, only that in Mummy Cave was in a ceremonial chamber, or kiva. The symbolic meaning of any of them is uncertain. Over the course of years following the discoveries discussed herein, other traces of prehistoric painted walls have come to light across the Pueblo domain, some in kivas, some on exterior walls in protected places. Such decoration probably was a rather common feature, perhaps not always sacred, that has suffered the ravages of the elements or simply has not yet been encountered. First from Spanish accounts and later from ethnographic inquiries of the late nineteenth and early twentieth centuries, it is a practice known to have continued into the historic period. Today it is thought-provoking to observe imagery derived from the native iconography being applied by Indian artists in Catholic missions situated in various of the Pueblos. The Franciscan priests assigned in the seventeenth century to erect churches at Awatovi and Gran Quivera would have been aghast.

The accounts to follow review the discoveries of these remarkable works that only fortuitously survived for a half millennium. Their recordation, preservation, and current conditions comprise an important part of the history of Southwestern archaeology that is not readily available to persons outside of the profession. The work done in these sites also exemplifies the various ways in which archaeology has been accomplished. These include individual research; largescale, multidisciplinary expeditions by prestigious institutions; educational programs for college students; and government projects for taxpayers' benefit. Anglos, Hispanics, and Native Americans working together to unravel a past that in some way was part of the heritage of all reflect the layered ethnicity and cultural richness of this unique region. Their diverse social, economic, and academic underpinnings and their experiences add color to their chronicle. We go behind the scenes, or more appropriate to this theme, behind the walls to savor some of those kinder, gentler eras when they were active. These were four decades (1930s–1960s) bridging earlier ones when the profession's emphasis was on the gathering of things and the establishment of a chronology and those later ones characterized by entanglements with abstract models pertaining to the "new archaeology." There were far fewer professionally trained individuals in the field then than now, and they were free to employ helpers from local communities who lacked that experience. To some degree there was a sense of adventure that is missing in today's greater familiarity with the territory and its past human history. They also were times when wall paintings were art and the ancient peoples of the Colorado Plateau were Anasazi.

A word needs to be said about those words. Some persons who enjoy dueling with semantics object to the use of the word *art* in describing prehistoric images put on the faces of cliffs and walls. They reason that artistic creativity was not their purpose but graphic expression of inner prayers or sacred visions was. These purists also reject the term *Anasazi* because it is Navajo and therefore not relevant to Pueblo culture. To heed these views, I have assiduously attempted to find substitutions and hope mental lapses will be forgiven. I am, after all, from those kinder, gentler epochs.

With archaeologists hopefully appeased, I have tried to avoid criticism from artists by not calling the Pueblo wall imagery frescos. True frescos are paintings in watercolors over wet plaster concocted from lime and sand. The works considered here were done on dry adobe and sand plaster occasionally washed with a thin gypsum coating. Hence they were not incorporated into the plaster layer but rode on its surface. They were more vulnerable to attack by destructive forces because of that. *Fresco seco* is sometimes used to denote such a technique but is not part of this text because, to me, it implies a formally contrived outlet for preconceived patterning lacking spontaneity.

In the Old World frescos appeared as early as the Egyptian kingdoms and the technique was also practiced by Minoans, Romans, Etruscans, and others. It reached its climax during the European Renaissance, coincidentally the same centuries when Pueblo artists were at work before their walls. In both cases walls were used as instruments for religious expression but by different methods and with different results each of which mirrored the cultural milieu from which they came. It is not my intention here to interpret that of the Pueblos beyond a few highlights of special interest. As archaeologists worked with ancestral Pueblo murals, they became increasingly cognizant of their sensitive nature and the need to treat them respectfully as part of the sacred patrimony of Native American groups. That approach has guided the subject matter in this book.

Most of the individuals mentioned herein were my friends during various of the sixty years I have been on the sidelines envious of their exciting endeavors. One was my husband. They gave me pleasure. They gave us all knowledge. For both reasons, I salute them with gratitude.

One of the pleasures of research such as this is having the sincere cooperation and help of so many professional guardians of our heritage and others who share a taste for the past and adventures to retrieve it. Among the first group my heartfelt thanks go to Tracy Murphy, Tony Marinella, and David Wilcox of the Museum of Northern Arizona; to Marian Rodee and Todd Lamkin of the Maxwell Museum; to Todd Ellison and Catherine Conrad of the Center of Southwest Studies, Fort Lewis College; to Susan Thomas and Victoria Atkins of the Anasazi Heritage Center; to Kristie Arrington of the Bureau of Land Management, and to Curtis Schaafsma, Diane Bird, and Lou Ann Haecker of the Laboratory of Anthropology. In the midst of their own busy routines, they all went out of their ways to facilitate my endeavors. Other colleagues whom I am proud to call friends and who were especially helpful are Richard Woodbury, Caroline Olin, Carol Harrison, David Stuart, Jerry and Jean Brody, Patricia Vivian, Ellen Abbott Kelley, and Anne Woolsey. Most of all, I was so fortunate to have thoughtful consultation with Gwinn Vivian, Alden Hayes, and David Breternitz without whom much of the background spirit and many old photographs could not have been had. A nod of appreciation also to Robert Jensen whose skill brought faded images back to life. Finally, above all, I am deeply indebted to Ruth Slickman — traveling companion, tireless photographer, and a lady of enviable humor, grace, and intellect.

High Noon at Lowry

Among the things they don't tell you until you have committed funds and energy to becoming a professional archaeologist is the fact that field-work can be hazardous to your health and peace of mind. Take, for instance, bandits with a callous disregard for life and limbs (yours!), wild animals, wary natives, research grants in foreign currency that becomes worthless overnight, rapacious bureaucrats trained to misplace your required official documents until a satisfactory bribe is forthcoming, or infectious tropical diseases for which there is no known cure. Of course, all these things can, and do, happen in distant exotic lands. But a deadly ambush on the Great Sage Plain of southwestern Colorado? Until a recent fruitless manhunt in the area for several killers, it would have seemed unlikely.

Yet that is the way Paul Martin remembered it.[1] Assistant curator of archaeology at the Denver Museum and, after 1930, at the Field Museum of Natural History in Chicago, Martin was a young man just beginning what was to become a long and distinguished career in Southwestern archaeology. He had come to this part of Colorado in 1930 to undertake his first big excavation at Lowry Ruin. A nearby settler named McKendry (or McKendree) Foster, mistakenly believing he owned the site and angry at this unwanted intrusion, in the dead of night broke the diggers' shovels and sawed their pickax handles in two. The next day when Martin confronted Foster about this vandalism, the irate settler ordered him off the property at gun point. Foster declared that he was going to fence the road to halt entry. To underscore his protest, Foster then took to aiming potshots at the workers, who wisely dove into their trenches. The climax came when Foster hid in a clump of brush and, as Martin drove past, jumped on the running board brandishing a piece of metal pipe in a most menacing manner. Martin recalled that he was terrified as he rolled across the seat and out the opposite car door. With the motor still running, he braced himself against the vehicle and aimed his gun at his assailant. Foster retreated in a rage. Martin slumped to his knees, thinking this was a rotten way to start a dig he had hoped would bring him fame and glory.

Watson Smith, a midwestern lawyer who was following a dream that summer by joining Martin's small expedition, remembered this skirmish differently.[2] He later wrote, "I don't remember at all anything about Paul carrying a gun; and it surprises me that he had to have a permit for one; I should have thought that in Montezuma County, whoever wanted to carry a gun could do so." In Watson's memoirs written sixty years after the fact, his version was that Martin's car had smashed a wooden cattle guard. In retaliation, Foster threw a barricade across the road and posted himself as an armed sentry.[3]

Regardless of which scenario is correct, the two frustrated would-be archaeologists sought the help of colleague Jesse Nusbaum, then director of the new Laboratory of Anthropology in Santa Fe. For the previous decade, Nusbaum had been superintendent at Mesa Verde National Park, which could be seen looming on the eastern horizon at Lowry Ruin. He knew the territory and perhaps even this unreasonable inhabitant. Nusbaum, in turn, called upon the agent for the regional Land Office to settle the dispute.

Technically Foster did not yet have title to his homestead because he had not done the required assessment improvements.[4] Furthermore, Lowry Ruin was on federal land, and Martin had a proper excavation permit. But rather than further muddle matters, the self-assured agent relied upon charm. He called upon Foster, sympathized with his hard lot on this unforgiving chunk of real estate, and sought to ingratiate himself by chopping wood. In the continuing cycle of bad luck, he broke the ax handle. Again Foster went for his gun, and the agent went for his car.

According to Smith, the final outcome of this ridiculous standoff caused by both parties' lack of understanding was that Martin's crew fixed the cattle guard. Meanwhile, Martin begrudgingly blazed a new, more circuitous, route to the site in order to avoid trespassing on Foster's future property. As Martin told it, he achieved a truce by buying the ruin and surrounding ten acres from Foster. Another version was that the Field Museum paid Foster forty dollars for the privilege of continuing excavations during the 1934 season and that two neighbors witnessed the written agreement because Foster could neither read nor write.[5] However the affair ended, in print Martin was gracious enough to say the incident was settled "amicably and expeditiously,"[6] words that his adversary would never read. The trouble might have been avoided had Martin taken the time to meet Foster on friendly terms and explain the value of his research. By not doing so, he came across to this uneducated man striving just to find a life for himself and his family as arrogant and thoughtless. Expectedly, Foster responded by resorting to the law of the Old West: firepower.

The area where the Battle of Lowry Ruin occurred was a large tract west of the tiny farming community of Cortez, Colorado, which the government opened for homesteading shortly before and after World War I. Most of those who settled there were resilient, God-fearing, hard-working, poorly educated, politically conservative, good-hearted frontier stock. Their primary assets were stern wills, stout backs, and firm determinations to make a living off the land. Although they spread widely across the virgin countryside, they developed a staunch mutual bonding through shared hardships and social and economic status that made them suspicious of outsiders from other backgrounds.

As the homesteaders set about erecting tarpaper shacks and sod houses and laboriously clearing the land, they encountered frequent evidence that these plains once had been occupied by many others. Who they were and why or when they left was unknown and seemingly of little interest. Craggy heaps of stones from fallen structures thickly dotted the open terrain and crowded into alcoves weathered into sheer stony escarpments of the region's many deep, dissecting canyons. Farmers plowed up numerous small mounds in their fields but left others as sagebrush-covered islands. For some, the ruins were yet another annoying obstacle to development. For others, they were a curiosity, perhaps places to pass a few hours on Sunday afternoons moseying around for pieces of pottery, stone tools, or other relics that ended up on dusty shelves or were tossed aside with the trash. One exception was a man named Courtney Dow who contacted the Denver Museum of Natural History about a ruin on his property that he thought might have scientific value.[7] He claimed to have mapped three hundred sites in the area. It was into this cultural climate, and as a result of Dow's notification, that Paul Martin had arrived at Lowry Ruin (Fig. 1). All odds were against his being readily accepted. He was not only an outsider but, after he moved back to his hometown of Chicago, was considered as being from the big city "back east." He was an urban elitist amidst humble land grubbers, a professional man driving a large Pierce Arrow canvas-topped touring car while the locals got around in horse-drawn wagons or in flivvers. Moreover, he was being paid for a kind of work the struggling homesteaders must have viewed as incomprehensible, if not meaningless.

Field arrangements beneficial to several of the neighbors softened some of the inherent resentment. The depth of the Great Depression and always chancy dry farming had left many families virtually destitute. For them several summer months of work and payment in hard cash, which Martin secured from the Montezuma County Emergency Relief Administration for a digging crew, meant sheer survival. Eager workers who already knew how to handle shovels and picks with hardened hands, could drive a team of animals, and did not have to be fed and lodged at night were to Martin's great advantage. Old photos show them in the

Fig. 1. Paul S. Martin.

rural garb of the times: bib overalls, heavy-soled work shoes, and broad-brimmed straw hats. In contrast, the professionals of the day were apt to appear in what was considered the appropriate costume of knee-high laced boots and riding britches.

There were at least two negative factors associated with poking around the ancient stony heaps, but neither of them was directly related to the ruins themselves or stopped their exploration. For one thing, late spring or early summer in this area typically sees an infestation of annoying gnats called no-see-ums. They swarm around ears, eyes, hair, ankles, and any exposed body parts in between. Their bites cause red welts and extreme itching. Some people have severe reactions; others are simply miserable. In the 1930s when Martin was there, insect repellant — still not very effective against these pests — was totally unknown. A second potential hazard was, and still is, the rattlesnakes, which seem to find comfort in the warmth of stone walls. The probability of chance encounters with them is slim, but a digger must be alert.

Fig. 2. Martin's log cabin and tent camp near Lowry Ruin.

Al Lancaster was one of the homesteaders hired by Martin. He was a strong, hard worker who had done manual labor in the region for at least a decade and had acquired a host of practical skills that would prove valuable in conducting field archaeology. He also possessed a rare intuitive sense about antiquities that would sustain him for an incredible future of seventy years in archaeological fieldwork. After one learning season, he became Martin's dig boss and unknowingly was launched on a successful career that took him out of the bean fields of southwestern Colorado.

Two other local residents, the Clyde Long couple, gained in a different way. For a half dozen seasons Martin rented their three-room log cabin as his headquarters (Figs. 2–4). During these times, they moved out and bedded down in an outbuilding. The wife cooked for Martin and the few other "outsiders" who had been imported for special tasks and stayed in a tent in the yard. The husband did odd carpentry and handyman jobs for the project. Income from the sacrifices and services

*Fig. 3. The Field Museum expedition shower: bucket
overhead, tub below.*

must have been welcome to the Longs, and the activities and personalities of their visitors must have fueled many a winter's conversation.

Martin had chosen a career for which, in part, he was neither physically nor emotionally fit. He learned firsthand about health hazards by contracting malaria, worms, and amoebic dysentery while employed at his first scientific job at the great Maya city of Chichen Itza in Yucatan.

Fig. 4. Entrance to photographic darkroom built into side of root cellar at the Field Museum camp.

As a result, he was sickly for the rest of his life, requiring a special diet. He also deplored the usual discomforts associated with fieldwork, feeling that he was "civilized" and deserved creature comforts. Smith recalled that at Lowry each morning Martin drove the resident personnel to the site in his cumbersome Pierce Arrow, outlined the day's program, then returned to the cabin. There he put some records of classical music on his portable phonograph and settled down to consideration of his excavation notes. After lunch came the afternoon nap. In late day he returned to the dig, inspected work accomplished, and drove the crew back to the cabin. Smith was flabbergasted that this leader of the project did not put in more than an hour a day at the site yet seemed to know exactly what was unfolding.[8] However, Martin's unconventional version of archaeology by remote control was so successful that his legacy is still highly respected. Lowry essentially was a one-man affair, although Martin did entertain Lawrence Roys, an architect, at the site for a short time.

In the final report, an appendix on the recovered skeletal remains was provided by an assistant professor at the University of Illinois, Gerhardt von Bonin. Today even a site of moderate size such as Lowry proved to be would require the combined expertise of at least a half dozen experts.

Lowry Ruin is a derelict ancestral Pueblo settlement nine miles out on the plateau extending southwest of the town of Pleasant View, to the west of Cortez. When Martin first saw the ruin in 1928, it was a thirty-foot-high earthen pile with scattered sagebrush, stones from collapsed walls, and a peppering of broken pieces of pottery. From its crest one could luxuriate in views of vast slices of the Colorado Plateau, its lofty mountains in all four directions, tablelands down below mantled in places with evergreens, and just to the west a canyon carving southward toward the San Juan River. In 1930 Martin began excavations with two long trenches to define the outline of the building that he felt lay under the surface. As work continued, Martin was certain that a pithouse hamlet of several rooms and probably of eighth-century age had been on the knoll over which the larger settlement was constructed. His crew did not explore that possibility but instead exposed a later linear structure of approximately forty rooms, some of which were on two or perhaps three levels. The dirt that had drifted over the old house as it sank in on itself like a deflated balloon was shoveled out by the workmen to where others guiding a scraper pulled by a team of horses or a mine car on tracks could remove it to a dump.[9] These were standard field methods of the era. Judging from wall abutments and bonding, Martin believed the houseblock had grown in five increments, with periods of abandonment in between, and that the total occupation had been no more than three or four decades spanning the end of the eleventh and the early twelfth centuries. He identified three kinds of masonry techniques: one using thin, flat, shaped tablets and spalls of a rust-colored sandstone facing a rubble core; one using a light-colored blocky sandstone without the hearting; and one that was a combination of the two other methods. He termed the first variation Chaco-like.[10]

Among the most interesting features of the site were four circular kivas, or ceremonial rooms, incorporated in or near the houseblock and having some walls that were partially painted. All were of what later researchers would regard as a typical style of the Mesa Verde province of the ancestral Pueblos. That is, they exhibited tall, spaced, masonry pillars seated on low encircling benches that had supported a cribbed-beam roof construction, had sets of horizontal pole shelving embedded between them, and had a projecting floor-level alcove on the south side.

The kiva containing the best-preserved example of mural painting was buried beneath an identical chamber on the upper story. When the excavators finished clearing out the upper kiva, they broke through its earthen floor and discovered the lower example. Over time that chamber had partially filled with windblown earth and trash. At some point occupants of the site had removed the roof beams to be used elsewhere, and the naked walls of sandstone and puddled adobe had soon begun to wear down. Later inhabitants leveled the spot and erected a duplicate, but slightly larger, kiva on top of it. The explanation for this building sequence of one kiva above another will always be elusive, but it was a fortunate occurrence for modern observers because the fill below helped to keep intact the painted wall of the lower kiva.

The walls of the upper unit (Kiva A) were sandstone blocks. Its bench face bore twenty-five coats of plaster but, having been exposed to centuries of weathering, these were in an extremely fragile state.[11] Excavators noted earlier drawings on an underlying plaster layer in this upper kiva. They were repeated brown rectangles in one row that were topped with white dots.[12]

The lower unit (Kiva B) had walls of tabular sandstone, and there were eight layers of plaster on the bench front. Martin's report does not indicate any special approach to cleaning the fill away from the plaster except, one would assume, extreme caution.

The face of the two-foot-high encircling bench, or banquette, of the lower kiva had been smoothed with dark brown adobe plaster over which were painted two decorative bands defined in white and carrying white patterns. The design elements were inch-wide, diagonal, five-terrace lines separated by vertical lines. The two bands were offset so that the vertical dividers did not match up. Whether or not the motif had symbolic meaning is unknown, but certainly that would have been appropriate for enhancement of a place where religious rituals were performed. Today Pueblo informants generally interpret terraced elements as representing clouds.

The diggers excavated two sections of this kiva. These units were sufficient to show that the mural continued around the entire bench. There was evidence of at least two decorated layers beneath the surface one, but no attempt was made to expose them. The project photographer took a number of pictures at floor level and from above peering down into the kiva. No scale drawings were made. Perhaps, since the design was simple and repetitive, that was not deemed necessary.

Fearing that the delicate wall paintings would disintegrate more than they had prior to excavation, Martin had his crew paint eight coats of clear shellac over a portion of the wall in the lower unit, Kiva B. When that coating dried and an underground ventilator shaft was reroofed, he directed that the kiva be promptly filled again with sterile soil. Kiva A also was backfilled.

Although Martin's report to the Department of the Interior, one sponsor of the project, was that the work of his crew was so skillfully carried out that not a single stone fell from the towering walls of the upper kiva into the seventeen-foot-deep lower kiva, there had been a scare that was behind the urgency to fill in the kivas.[13] Lancaster and a helper barely managed to scramble out of a deep trench along the exterior west side of the kivas before a great portion of upper wall came thundering down. It obliterated their efforts, buried their hastily discarded shovels, and easily could have crushed them.[14]

Even though these painted walls at Kiva B had suffered some damage before excavation, they were special because of their extent. Furthermore, three other kivas within the houseblock or nearby had fragmentary evidence of the same treatment in what must have been a local idiosyncrasy. During the half century that archaeologists previously had explored ancient Pueblo ruins of the northern Southwest, they had discovered patches of painted walls, primarily interior surfaces but, in rare protected situations, also exterior surfaces. They were most commonly associated with sites in the Mesa Verde province, such as those at Cliff Palace in Mesa Verde National Park, and within the same time frame as Lowry Ruin. The paintings were monochromatic, and most of them were geometric in nature. The carryover from pottery design was obvious. Occasionally walls bore elements duplicating those on contemporaneous pottery imagery, such as birds, quadrupeds, or flute players. However, no murals then known compared in concentration at one site or in scope with those at Lowry Ruin. In four field seasons (during 1930–1931 and 1933–1934) the project for which Martin was responsible had made a significant discovery. It was not one that homesteader Foster would have appreciated but certainly one of value to science. Curiously, Martin did not mention it in his reminiscences about the site, as though he too did not really grasp the importance that years later would lead to the fruitless expenditure of thousands of government dollars in an attempt to preserve it.[15]

With the exception of the earliest design layer in Kiva A, the remaining elements mirrored those on concurrent Mesa Verde regional pottery, although in a negative rather than positive way. Art historian J. J. Brody sees these kivas as architectural translations of those ceramics in being round as bowls with banded geometric patterning on their interiors.[16] Through analogy with historic practices, scientists regard the ancestral Pueblo women as the potters in terms of both vessel formation and decoration. Does that mean that women painted the Lowry kivas? Probably not. Again in an analogous explanation based on the historic Pueblo situation, the kiva was a male sanctuary and, one might conclude, was thus decorated by men. Furthermore, the geometric design vocabulary was the common tribal predilection that was used and applied in various media by both sexes.

Because of the masonry style Martin termed Chaco-like and the presence of an associated Great Kiva and road segments, many of today's researchers classify Lowry Ruin as a Chaco outlier on the most distant northwestern frontier of the ancestral Pueblo domain. It may be more correct to think of it as some ill-defined Chaco influence that reached this region, rather than as any actual migration of Chacoans to the Great

Sage Plain. Some substantiation for this opinion is that three of the four painted kivas (A, B, D, and H) had walls of Chaco-like masonry but interior features like those of the Mesa Verde tradition and designs that were more like those of the bold, packed Mesa Verde style than like the frenetic, thin-lined hatchure typical of Chaco artisans at 1100.

During the course of Martin's work at Lowry, his workmen backfilled some rooms and capped the tops of walls for their protection. Sand, cement, and water to mix the mortar had to be brought from distant sources. Authorities at Mesa Verde National Park also loaned the services of one of the park's maintenance crew to pour cement capping over the tops of a few walls. Then the site sank back into quiet obscurity out beyond the bean fields and rapidly began to decay. As for Martin, after several seasons' additional brief forays, he gladly abandoned the Great Sage Plain and, like the prehistoric folks, went south.

The pile of dirt and plant life that had accumulated over the Lowry houseblock during the passage of centuries formed a hard rind that protected what lay beneath the surface. Once that rind was peeled away, the fragile structure was exposed to destructive elemental forces. Penetration of moisture from above and below caused unreinforced mud mortar to melt and porous sandstone to soften and even dissolve. Heaving from freezing and thawing activity dislodged building blocks. Water collected on low earthen floors. As thirty years of disinterest went by, twelfth-century Lowry Ruin and its associated Great Kiva were facing eradication.

Belatedly, the Bureau of Land Management, the federal agency having jurisdiction over Lowry Ruin, decided to open the site to the public. In 1965 the regional office contracted with the Mesa Verde Research Center, directed by Professor Robert Lister of the University of Colorado, to make necessary repairs. Lister hired Al Lancaster, recently retired from the National Park Service, to oversee the job. He had spent many years heading up a team of Navajos doing stabilization work at Mesa Verde National Park and was eminently qualified.

Lancaster recruited a crew of his former helpers. They reset walls that had slumped, capped others with cement, replaced wooden lintels,

Fig. 5. Rooms at south end of Lowry Ruin, through which painted Kiva B later would be reached, prior to stabilization, 1964.

sloped floors for drainage, removed fallen debris, and paid particular attention to the Great Kiva in a depression to the east of the houseblock that captured runoff (Fig. 5). Bureau of Land Management workers built tourist facilities. One was a self-guiding trail around the perimeter of the site along which workmen placed informative markers at specific places of interest. The one at Kiva A noted that buried below it was a similar chamber having an especially fine mural panel.

In October 1967 this nine-hundred-year old village became a National Historic Landmark celebrated by festivities attended by Bureau of Land Management officials and Al Lancaster. An Indian dance team from Fort Lewis College in Durango performed in the plaza.[17] What was to become its most unique feature remained obscured.

Any student of human nature should have realized that the notice on the surface above Kiva B would provoke an outcry for making it available for viewing. The predictable script went as follows: the site is on public lands; taxpayers have a right to know; archaeologists want to keep all the goodies to themselves; et cetera. After seven years of numerous protests from visitors, the Bureau of Land Management bowed to public demand just in time for the nation's Bicentennial. That was a fateful decision.

Once again, in 1974, the Mesa Verde Research Center, then directed by David Breternitz, was given the contract to undertake reopening Kiva B. It promised to be a demanding, costly, time-consuming excavation, stabilization, and engineering effort. Breternitz arranged with the University of Colorado to offer a graduate-level class in such archaeologically related enterprises. Although maintenance of excavated surface sites is a major problem in the Southwest, no university provided such instruction. The target in this instance was to be Lowry Ruin and the day-to-day guidance was to be provided by Al Lancaster. He had finished high school at the age of twenty-eight and gone no further with formal academic studies, but he had an unequaled field resume in this sort of work. He was then a vigorous seventy-eight years old.

The university group consisted of seven males and one or two females. Larry Nordby, E. Charles Adams, and Cory Breternitz were to continue careers in regional prehistory, with others like Adrian White in related roles. The party was not as fortunate in its camp as Martin had been. During the first four-week session in 1974, the crew set up cots in a musty abandoned farmhouse nearby. The cook had his own trailer. The next summer the students tented on Lancaster's farm and used his barn for a kitchen. As often happens in regional archaeology, the wife of one of them, Jennie Adams, was the cook.

Extensive attention was to be given to the entire prehistoric complex, but reopening Kiva B was the first goal. In order to clear the lower kiva, it was necessary to clean out the backfill in Kiva A and to dismantle its most threatening walls. Although removal of antiquities is counter to a discipline that emphasizes preservation, all but the west wall of Kiva A had deteriorated beyond salvation. Disposing of the accumulated soil and weeds that soon engulf an unused structure is always a field problem. Lancaster tried to use a wooden slide down the exterior west face of the houseblock into which such overburden could be dumped. It proved impractical because of damp soil. The slide was replaced by a wheelbarrow ramp across the second level to a spot where debris from Kiva A and that burying the first level could be deposited. Clearing efforts, as they had been for the first excavators, were strenuous because the depth of Kiva B meant handling the spoil dirt several times.[18] Fortunately, the kiva had not been sunk below outside ground level or the work would have been even more arduous.

What the most recent excavators found was that Martin's measures for preserving the Kiva B painted walls were not entirely successful.[19] The shellacked surfaces on about a third of the kiva had hardened, which had caused them to pull away from the stone walls behind. Roots, dirt, moisture, and salts leached from the masonry that worked down between layers promoted further separation. The stabilizers could see at least five plaster layers, with three probably decorated. However, the plaster was too soft to be scraped. When the mass dried through exposure, extensive crumbling was anticipated. The portions of the bench that had not been cleared in the 1930s remained in better but tenuous condition. Work to attempt protection of the entire kiva proceeded but with a general agreement among consulted archaeologists and ruins preservation specialists that the original mural likely could not be saved. An exact replication eventually would have to be drawn. To that end, the crew made careful tracings and photographs to be used for future reference. Once recording was completed, the painted walls were covered with plastic sheeting.[20]

The diggers recovered several wood samples from the kiva deposits, and the samples were submitted to the laboratory at the University of Arizona for tree-ring dating. The results indicated that construction of Kiva B had taken place about 1106. Kiva A, above, dated to 1120.[21] Martin believed Kiva B and several adjacent first-level rooms represented the second building episode at the site, perhaps fifteen years or so after the

Fig. 6. Kiva B, Lowry Ruin, being reopened and pilasters being rebuilt by University of Colorado students, 1975.

other occupants erected a four-room unit to the north. Considering the debris that Martin's group removed from Kiva B, it must have been abandoned and left open for a few years before Kiva A (with twenty-five coats of plaster) was put on top of it during a third construction expansion. Further, the four layers of plaster the students counted under the remaining outer one at Kiva B suggested that the chamber had been used for some time prior to the final painting. Therefore, the last mural may have been painted about 1115.

Seven students were each assigned the task of rebuilding one of the Kiva B pilasters in order to bring them back to a height sufficient to support a new roof. They used shaped stones fallen in other parts of the ruin and laid them up in colored cement mortar. They mudded joints with soil cement to make repair work as inconspicuous as possible. The fill between two pilasters was left in place to buttress old construction on the upper level. Each pilaster reflected the individual workmanship, as must have been the case in the original construction (Fig. 6).

While Lancaster was overseeing this work, he had a second Lowry mishap. He lost his balance at the upper edge of Kiva B and fell headlong into the deep pit. A student managed to grab his jacket just enough to break what could have been a fatal impact. Lancaster lay spread-eagled on the kiva floor for a few moments. Then he raised his hand to signal that he was all right and admonished the worried crew, "Don't tell my wife!"[22]

As the 1975 season got underway, a second contingent of students removed the temporary tarpaper and corrugated tin roof that had covered the kiva for the previous winter. It was replaced by a permanent layered roof of heavy rafters, plywood, tarpaper, and soil that extended over Kiva B and an adjoining room. The ancestral Pueblo roof had been of cribbed logs. Rather than copy that style, Lancaster and Breternitz hoped the beam rafters would impart something of the same effect. Two plastic skylights were secured in the roof to light the areas below. A drain box at one side connected to a vertical plastic pipe was meant to carry off unwanted water that might collect on the roof. In the twelfth century, access to the chamber had been by means of a ladder through a central smoke hole in the roof. That was not acceptable in this instance because of possible damage to the paintings below due to natural or human causes. Workers prepared a new ground-level entry through a room at the east side of the houseblock. Visitors could come by way of two reconstructed rooms (numbers 9 and 27 in Martin's report) into the southern recess, closed off from the kiva proper by a low metal gate, and peer into the kiva. At last they were able to stand before the painted walls and, it was hoped, have some appreciation for the sanctity of the surroundings to the early inhabitants (Fig. 7). However, Bureau of Land Management satisfaction with the improvements was short lived.

Very soon half the plaster in Kiva B flaked off to the floor or separated

Fig. 7. Kiva B, Lowry Ruin, after reexcavation and stabilization, 1976.

and hung precariously away from the supporting walls. Large white splotches were left where brown adobe had been, making the mural face appear to be disfigured from some awful skin disease (Fig. 8).

Consequently, two years after the stabilization work, the administrators concluded that something had to be done to hold the paintings in place if at all possible. They sought the help of William Burke, a chemist on the faculty of Arizona State University. He had some experience in preserving rock art panels with a chemical solution that had as its main ingredient methyl methacrylate. In the fall of 1977 Burke and his assistant Rick Bradshaw came to Lowry to experiment with possible ways of securing the panels. First they cleaned the walls. Then they used heat lamps to bring the temperature of the test patches up to 100 degrees. They covered the spots with hardware cloth sprayed with three gallons of their special preservative and allowed these tests to cure untouched

*Fig. 8. Kiva B, Lowry Ruin, showing deterioration of painted banquette
in 1980s.*

for an hour. In a second experiment, the men substituted a heater for the
lamps and placed an electric blanket on the panels during the curing
process.[23] In the end, the experiments were unsuccessful. The chemicals penetrated and hardened the plaster so that it could be scraped but
failed to bond plaster to wall. The murals continued to disintegrate into
fragments that were larger and harder than formerly.

Meanwhile bureaucratic in-fighting and inertia and changes in personnel and policy delayed any positive action to remedy the situation.
Rootlets and atmospheric conditions took their toll.

Finally facing up to the problem, the Bureau of Land Management
contracted with a professional conservator. This was Constance Silver,
who had a background in Southwestern archaeology and some prior
training in Europe in mural preservation. Her experience with true

fresco actually was going to be of limited value in coping with thin gypsum paint over naked, hardened mud plaster. However, she put in three stints from 1981 through 1983 at Lowry. Upon viewing the situation for the first time, Silver was filled with mixed emotions of dismay, frustration, and anger over what she considered carelessness in procedures and fundamental disinterest in effective protection of the valuable resource the murals represented. In her reports she recited a long litany of complaints.[24] Although the roof beams lent a feeling compatible with the original cribbed construction, they were too heavy for the tops of unstable walls. They caused buckling of walls and the plaster upon them. The roof also leaked, allowing water, the primary enemy of unreinforced adobe, to run down behind and over the various coats. The chamber enclosure itself let humidity build so that evaporation of moisture was curtailed. The ground-level entry promoted harmful drafts. And most annoying of all was slow action by government employees in fixing the troublesome roof. She felt that she had done her best to hold off total disaster until she could return the next summer, better prepared to make necessary repairs.

On her return Silver found the conditions worse than before. After due time, the authorities had heeded her warning about the porous roof and had hired a contractor to remove and replace it with a different style of construction that inevitably was more costly. However, once the roof was off, the contractor abruptly declared that funding was inadequate. He irresponsibly walked off the job, leaving the kiva open to the sky for the winter. The following summer Silver and her assistant encountered saturated walls and a large mud puddle on the kiva floor. Sections of plaster were just dangling. Mold had formed on some surfaces. Salts appeared near the soil line. In an attempt to protect the exposed paintings, monument workers had piled insulation next to the bench. Unfortunately, that material retained moisture. Worse yet, as far as the two women were concerned, it attracted an infestation of rats that chewed on it, nested in it, clawed the soft plaster, deposited their feces on the bench top, and left permanent urine stains on the murals. One is reminded of an old Indiana Jones movie with rats swarming around an archaeological treasure. It was not that repulsive, but the women must have wondered for a time just why they were in this line of work.

Despite their wariness, Silver and her helper set about scraping off the mud and dirt that obscured some of the painted surfaces. They removed the objectionable insulation and the rodent droppings. Cautiously they covered the painted walls with Japanese tissue dampened with water, alcohol, and chemicals. By hand they pushed loosened plaster back onto the masonry, hoping they had found an adequate adhesive. Where possible, they followed the same procedure with pieces picked up from the floor. They coated exposed edges of mortar and the few original shelving poles between pilasters with preservatives. As a final step, they draped nylon sheeting and bubble wrap over the panels and stacked sandbags in front to hold the materials in place.

By the 1983 season, a new roof and vertical metal girders to help support it were installed. Still, the cycle of erosion was too far advanced to be stalled. Silver saw no alternative but to put a pegboard coated with soil and vermiculite in front of the nylon sheeting covering the panels. In effect, it was meant to serve the same purpose as the Martin backfill of a half century before. The panels themselves could no longer be viewed, making interpretation for visitors difficult.

Four years later, in 1987, the Bureau of Land Management undertook additional efforts to save the murals. This time they turned to the Rocky Mountain Regional Conservation Center at Denver University. These experts reported that the pegboard frame had become waterlogged and warped, its backfill was wet, and the changes had left sizable portions of the panels unprotected. The men charged that had the Silver backfill been properly maintained, the lower portions of the panels likely would not have disappeared because of groundwater capillary action, nor would the rest of them have become so loosened that exfoliation was predictable. As it was, without further funding and, it was implied, more dedicated Bureau of Land Management commitment, they recommended that two representative pieces of the wall bearing decoration be salvaged and that the remainder of the painting be left to its ultimate fate.[25]

Fig. 9. Aerial view of Lowry Ruin after excavation and stabilization, 1976:
Great Kiva at left center; houseblock with roofed kiva at center.

Other than a few indistinguishable patches of plaster, today essentially all that remains of a wall painting nine hundred years old is a jagged
chunk in a glass case at the Anasazi Heritage Center in Dolores, Colorado. It is a pitiful display in front of a large reproduction of how it appeared when left by the ancestral Pueblos. It self-destructed within a
decade because of being removed from its protective environment. Bureau of Land Management workers place a small replication within the
kiva during periods of high visitation.

Hindsight now leads some observers to argue that reexcavation of
Kiva B should never have been done. Scientists and the public should
have been content with Martin's notes and photographs. Those involved
in the decision to reopen the kiva should have realized that multiple layers of plaster in it confirmed that the Pueblo artisans had had to cope

with the same destructive forces, in addition to smoke blackening from hearth fires and wear and tear from usage. If excavation was deemed vital, conservation methods should have been tested and readied before any digging was undertaken. That not having been done, many hours of labor and huge sums of money were wasted, and an important exhibit of prehistoric art and thought irrevocably vanished. In this engagement, the second Battle of Lowry Ruin ended in a conservation rout (Fig. 9).

The Lowry mural is literally a thing of the past, but visitors to the Anasazi Heritage Center, the Bureau of Land Management museum, can admire it in a fine CD-ROM "reenactment" prepared by programmers Theresa Brezau and Clay Hamilton. Viewers can visually descend into the decorated chamber to witness youngsters playing a game, a man sitting before his vertical loom, and a boy being taught how to shape a stone skinning knife. Re-creation of rituals for which the kiva was primarily intended is purposefully avoided.

Site managers are hopeful that a new cribbed shell meant to hide the free-standing roof superstructure will solve the periodic seepage problem and provide the room with a more authentic appearance.

Notes

1. Martin, 1974, 8.
2. Smith letter to Al Lancaster, October 29, 1974 (Archives, Fort Lewis College, Center of Southwest Studies, Durango, Colorado).
3. Smith, 1992, 115–121; Smith, n.d., 13–30.
4. R. M. Daly, Acting Special Agent in Charge of Investigations, Santa Fe, New Mexico, memorandum to A. C. Kinsley, Special Agent, Montrose, Colorado, June 26, 1933, Department of the Interior (Archives, The Field Museum, Chicago, Illinois); Martin, 1936, 14.
5. Agreement and receipt, July 1934 (Archives, The Field Museum, Chicago, Illinois).
6. Martin, 1936, 14.
7. J. L. Adams, 1994, 25; Martin, 1936, 16.
8. Smith, 1992, 115–121; Smith, n.d., 13–30.
9. Martin, 1936, 23, Pls. II, VI–VIII; Martin, 1974, 9–10; Martin letter to

S. C. Simms, Director, Field Museum of Natural History, July 12, 1930 (Archives, The Field Museum, Chicago, Illinois).

10. Martin, 1936, 28, 119–120, Pls. XXII–XXVI.

11. Ibid., Pls. XLVIII, LI, LVIII, LIX.

12. Ibid., Pl. LX.

13. Martin letter to John H. Edwards, Assistant Secretary, Department of the Interior, January 3, 1932 (Archives, Mesa Verde Research Center, Dove Creek, Colorado).

14. J. L. Adams, 1994, 28; Breternitz, personal communication.

15. Martin, 1974, 3–32.

16. Brody, 1991, 67–68.

17. Field notes, October 3, 1967 (Archives, Mesa Verde Research Center, Dove Creek, Colorado).

18. For a detailed account of the stabilization process, see White and Breternitz, 1976.

19. Bureau of Land Management report, December 1977 (Archives, Mesa Verde Research Center, Dove Creek, Colorado).

20. White and Breternitz, 1976, 24, Fig. 16.

21. Ibid., 5.

22. Breternitz, personal communication.

23. Bureau of Land Management report, December 1977 (Archives, Mesa Verde Research Center, Dove Creek, Colorado).

24. Silver, 1983 reports (Archives, Anasazi Heritage Center, Dolores, Colorado).

25. Charles Patterson, Objects Conservator, Rocky Mountain Regional Conservation Center, Report to Bureau of Land Management, RMRCC 87-321, May 1987, Denver, Colorado (Archives, Anasazi Heritage Center, Dolores, Colorado).

Did Coronado Sleep Here?

Francisco Vásquez de Coronado and his entourage arrived in the central Rio Grande valley of New Mexico in 1540, just twenty years after the mighty Aztec Empire had been brought down. Not invited, they nevertheless stayed for two winters, during which time they became very unwelcome guests, pillaging towns, murdering the residents, and trying to convince the locals that the Spanish way was the best in all regards. Although Spanish scribes noted between twelve and seventeen pueblos in the area, the names they used are unfamiliar today, and modern-day historians have been at a loss to know just which pueblo, if any, was where the invaders made themselves at home. At home, that is, by ousting Indian families from their hearths, confiscating food and other goods, and moving in. Separating fact from fiction being grist to the mill of historical determinations, those concerned individuals were restless until the question of Coronado's encampment was answered.

To identify the campsite as part of the upcoming observances of the four hundredth anniversary of the Coronado *entrada*, in 1934 Edgar Hewett launched an archaeological campaign (Fig. 10). Then in the twi-

Fig. 10. Edgar Lee Hewett, 1936.

light of a productive half century in which he had played a major role in numerous activities revolving around New Mexico's heritage, Hewett envisioned actually tracking down Coronado's camp. To be able to proclaim it as the place where the Spanish colonial history of New Mexico began would be a fitting climax to his life's work. Having established the Museum of New Mexico and the School of American Research some years before and the Department of Anthropology at the University of New Mexico in 1928, all of which he served simultaneously as head, he put his troops to work.

Locating promising sites in what was known as the Tiguex province, because of the presence of Tiwa speakers, was made difficult for the researchers by the construction methods of ancient builders. In a region short on immediately available stone, they had resorted to sun-dried adobe balls set up in copious mud mortar. When left untended, walls erected of these materials melted like chocolate over heat into puddles that hardened into clods. Additionally, in order to bring the natives to heel, the Spaniards had burned and otherwise destroyed their dwellings. Added to that devastation, and otherwise obscuring archeological clues, was the non-Indian exploitation of that sector of the Rio Grande valley since 1700, as well as the founding of Albuquerque.

One hopeful place to explore was a heap of worn-down adobe walls barely poking above a ground strewn with fragments of pottery bearing glaze-line decorations of a type considered by scientists to be a sixteenth-century style. Locally called Puaray, the site was situated on a gravel bench along the west bank of the Rio Grande opposite the small community of Bernalillo. Out farther to the west stretched a bleak mesa country with little vegetation and no water, a high desert to modern observers. The river bottomlands to the east just below the settlement could have been used for flood-water or irrigated farming. The setting seemed to fit descriptions in colonial accounts of a possible locale where the Spaniards were temporarily billeted, if not those in the Coronado party perhaps those in the expeditions that came north from Mexico toward the end of the century.

Aided as Martin was at Lowry Ruin by depression-era emergency relief funds (FERA) to hire a local digging crew, overseen by museum staff and advanced university students, excavation of what became identified as Bandelier's Puaray commenced as soon as winter broke in 1934, and work continued through the year. In the late nineteenth century, Adolph Bandelier, newly intrigued by Southwestern prehistory, had traveled the region, delved into old chronicles, and considered this site as having been that of Coronado's encampment.

Here, as at Lowry, the problem of operating a field camp was bypassed. Hewett's laborers went back at night to their Bernalillo homes across the river, and the staff and students returned to their quarters in Albuquerque just twenty miles to the south. Urban or semi-urban archaeology does have its advantages.

Puaray proved to be the ruins of four houseblocks of more than 450 contiguous, square, adobe-walled rooms arranged in honeycomb fashion around a central courtyard containing a single large round kiva. Marjorie Tichy, one of the dig supervisors, suggested that a somewhat different and larger structure off to one side of the complex might have been a chapel erected by the Spaniards, but it was too ruined for certain identification.[1]

As anticipated, researchers ascribed the pottery to the sixteenth and first half of the seventeenth centuries. No tree-ring dates were obtained. The exact date at which the town had been abandoned was not ascertained, but in the opinion of these scholars it happened some time before the 1680 Pueblo Revolt that drove the hated Spaniards away for a little more than a decade. The few sherds of ceramic wares made in Mexico, some rusted metal implements and fragments (including a flake of gold leaf), and a tatter of possible armor could have been discarded along the valley at any time during at least a hundred-year period and could then have been picked up by Indian gleaners. Or there may have been a dump near the site that had been used by the invaders. Bones of domesticated sheep and a single peach pit suggest the latter explanation. Nevertheless, it would appear that Coronado himself may not have slept at Puaray. Moreover, continuing documentary research revealed that somewhere along the east side of the Rio Grande there had been another native settlement given the same name. That settlement was not located, presumably having been lost to progress. Wesley Bliss, then a university graduate student, was convinced that the Santa Fe Railroad had cut through the probable site of the "real" Puaray, because he picked up horse bones there that were deposited some two feet below the surface.[2]

At the same time work was going on at Puaray, Hewett initiated a second dig at a similar but larger neighboring ruin area spreading over a quarter of a mile along the west terrace of the Rio Grande. Again he was able to use local Hispanic laborers to do the heavy digging (Fig. 11). The place (site LA187 in the archaeological records) was recorded as Kuaua, a Tiwa term for Douglas fir. It overlooked the broad Rio Grande, always brown and never silver as in song, lined with a green riparian habitat for bird life that used the thread of river as a seasonal flyway north and south. Off to the east was the sweeping panorama of pinyon-covered foothills and watermelon-colored mountains — the Sandias at sunset. That same scene today attracts retirees and Intel employees to settle in congestion

Fig. 11. Excavators at work at Kuaua, 1935.

not too unlike that of the ancestral Pueblo houseblocks—but greater in number and without underground places of worship.

Early in the twentieth century Charles Lummis had dug in the southern portion of the site, but otherwise the region was generally untouched. As the 1930s work at Kuaua commenced, only low mounds no more than five to ten feet high identified the location. These excavations lasted for five seasons. Hewett himself was otherwise busy with his many administrative duties but engaged the services of a cadre of individuals, then at various stages of training, who later became important figures in American archaeology. These included, among others, J. Charles Kelley (Fig. 12), Gordon Vivian (Figs. 13, 14), Marjorie Tichy (Lambert) (Fig. 23), Bertha Dutton (Fig. 25), Wesley Bliss (Fig. 21), and Robert Lister (Fig. 22). They demonstrated that the site was originally a small village founded in the fourteenth century; the date was based on a black-on-white pottery

Fig. 12. J. Charles Kelley at work at Kuaua, 1935.

Fig. 13. Gordon Vivian, 1935.

Fig. 14. Gordon Vivian in the University of New Mexico field vehicle, ca. 1934–1935.

Fig. 15. Partially cleared rooms, Kuaua, 1935.

decorative tradition determined by pottery analysts to date from that period. The settlement grew during the fifteenth and early sixteenth centuries into a community of at least twelve hundred rooms enclosing two
spacious enclosed plazas with five subterranean kivas (Fig. 15). Some of
the structures may have stood three stories high. A secondary addition
was located at the northeast corner of the complex. The kivas were of particular interest because prior archaeological work in the northern Southwest showed that circular kivas had been typical of the Four Corners
ancestral Pueblos and those occupying more easterly regions and that
rectangular ritual chambers were erected by plateau tribes to the west
and south. From that, excavators assumed that some sort of cultural
interaction had taken place at Kuaua, because both styles were present.

That was to be confirmed at the beginning of the 1935 excavation season when dig boss Gordon Vivian, then on the museum staff while also
a graduate student at the University of New Mexico, put a laborer to work

opening a test trench in the south plaza of the settlement. Vivian's later report does not indicate why he chose that particular spot, but it does state that there were no surface indications of former occupation.[3] No wall remnants stuck up above the hard ground, and there was no depression hinting at a possible subterranean structure. However, at a depth of just two feet the workman hit the top of an eroded adobe wall. As he continued shoveling, Vivian spotted flecks of colored plaster being thrown into the wheelbarrow used to haul off spoil dirt. He quickly took over the clearing process, carefully scraping down a wall surface with his trowel, brushing it softly with a whiskbroom, then slowly chipping off a blank adobe coating. Only later would he realize that he actually had gone through seven undecorated layers. What he reached was a patch of wall on which was the unmistakable image of a human *hand*. A major find was made that blustery February day because of the serendipity that occasionally is the archaeologist's good fortune.

The discovery of a wall painting at a late prehistoric Pueblo site was not totally unexpected. In fact, among the compelling reasons behind these explorations were accounts by some Spanish scribes of houses to the south of the Tiguex province having images of horrific "fierce and terrible demons" and "monsters." Translated that means figures puzzling to the invaders—figures unlike the bloody, agonized Jesuses nailed to a cross that were an integral part of the religious art of Spanish Catholicism. One particularly intriguing notation was made by Captain Gaspar Pérez de Villagrá, who served as scribe for conqueror Juan de Oñate in 1598. His account, written ten years later, describes a wall scene depicting the stoning and beating deaths of two Franciscans. These figures had disappeared following a 1581 expedition into New Mexico and were presumed to have been killed in the legendary Puaray.[4] Could this hand at the Kuaua kiva belong to one of them? To find the original painting and so verify an alleged historic event and to actually put the Spaniards at a settlement near Puaray would be an archaeological coup. But that was not to be.

Further clearing showed that the painted wall was part of a rectangular kiva. Although it had been primarily below the surface of the plaza when built, its superstructure might still have been in evidence had the upper courses not been so completely worn away. The painted hand belonged to a standing, white-bodied figure outlined in black with touches here and there of earth-red and wearing what was left of a horned, yellowish mask with an oval-shaped mouth. The figure's arms were bent upward at the elbows with hands raised, palms open (Fig. 16). It is identified by Zuni informants in the pantheon of Kuaua representations as Lu'kia, or dual personage, and as part of a panel of the ceremonial of the Sun Cult or history myth of the coming from the underworld.[5] Whether or not this interpretation is correct, the quaint little fellow always will have the distinction of being the first large-scale, multicolored wall image with humanlike characteristics discovered by regional archaeologists. In earlier times monochromatic figures had been painted on scattered ancestral Pueblo walls, but none were of this representational style nor in Rio Grande sites. The Kuaua discovery confirmed suspicions that figural wall painting indeed had been practiced by some early dwellers along the central Rio Grande valley of New Mexico.

In the weeks following this discovery, diggers learned that a somewhat larger kiva on the spot had been remodeled into a smaller version. Three walls of this later rectangular structure, indicated as Kiva III in the technical notes, had been decorated with what first impressed the excavators as representing a very long connection between past and present Pueblo ritualism in costuming and attitude. Only later would researchers consider the paintings as iconographic elements expressing religious dogma. The kiva's builders had reinforced a fourth wall by an interior secondary construction, destroying the designs on the original wall. From exposed edges of the accumulated plaster that was some two inches thick, Vivian concluded that the ancient artisans had applied numerous very thin adobe washes one on top of another, not all of which appeared to have been decorated. They faced structural walls of adobe balls in mud mortar that were approximately a foot and a half thick. Behind these was the undisturbed solid mesa into which the builders had sunk the shelter with the use of hardened sticks.

The young crew members, all of whom were virtual novices in the

*Fig. 16. First figure, in white with black outline, found on
outermost painted wall (Layer A-8) of Kiva III, Kuaua, 1935.*

finer techniques of their chosen craft, were exhilarated with what they
knew was a significant find. To be witness to a first was an unforgettable
way to begin a career. They also grew increasingly apprehensive that, in
the delicate recording and preservation process, they might unknowingly be responsible for some human or naturally caused damage. Some

plaster layers appeared to be separated from the structural wall and apt to fall. Collectively the crew worried about how they should go about peeling this aesthetic onion. How to get almost microscopically thin layers off and accounted for? What about those notorious New Mexico spring winds that carried heavy loads of sand that could pit the soft naked walls like an epidemic of smallpox? What if red-hot July heat dried them to the point of scaling, not necessarily in successive order? Summer showers could saturate and dissolve them into a muddy pudding (Fig. 17). And there was the ever-present possibility of after-hours prowlers unable to resist the temptation of adding initials to the motifs. Perhaps a night guard should be hired.

Naturally, for twenty-somethings this group consternation called for many evening beers at the student hangout across Central Avenue from the campus. Its name The Pig Stand added to its questionable allure. Perhaps it was this inimitable ambience and Budweiser that prompted Wesley Bliss's solution to the troubling problem. Why not do as the paleontologists do when they come across a hunk of dinosaur bone or other long-gone fossil, he asked. They encase the specimen in reinforced plaster-of-paris and cart it off to some laboratory where they can unwrap the package and examine it in controlled comfort. Just in case his listeners had forgotten, Bliss reminded them again that he had had such experience once as a student assistant.

Vivian thought this idea was wildly preposterous but that it just might work. He dashed off an urgent inquiry to conservators at the Fogg Art Museum at Harvard. Surely with all that institution's expertise there must be someone on the staff who knew whether or not jacketing the Kuaua kiva walls, removing them as entire blocks, and then recovering the contents stratum by stratum was either feasible or unmitigated madness. He got a prompt reply accompanied by an article in French dealing with the removal of Oriental frescos.[6] The advice was to go ahead but with extreme caution. Vivian put Bliss in charge. Doubtless this digger's surname reflected his state of mind.

Over dry plaster surfaces on the interior kiva walls and on an isolated decorated feature that the excavators thought to be an altar, Bliss and his

Fig. 17. Exposed mural on wall of Kiva III, Kuaua, under protection of a tent, 1935.

team painted white shellac or a liquid celluloid in order to harden them. They made scale drawings of the outer visible layer so as to ensure accurate reassemblage of separated walls. Then came applications of reams of tissue paper wet with water-soluble glue, plaster-of-paris, strips of muslin, lengths of lath reinforcing, and an outer timber framework in sections so that it could be removed later. Laborers opened trenches along the exterior kiva walls and built up a comparable strengthening shell of plaster-of-paris and muslin with a final heavy wooden frame that would

Fig. 18. *Jacketed walls of Kiva III, Kuaua, before being cut loose; still under cover of protective tent, 1935.*

Fig. 19. *Jacketed wall of Kiva III lifted out of kiva depression, 1935.*

Fig. 20. *Jacketed wall of Kiva III loaded on truck for transport to the University of New Mexico, 1935.*

serve as a solid background while study of the front surface was going on. Wall slabs, up to seven feet in height in some sections, were cut free at base and corners, sealed, and loaded by block and tackle onto vehicles loaned by the university motor pool (Figs. 18–20).[7] The altar, three-and-a-half feet long and two-and-a-half feet high, also was jacketed and removed.

One transport truck was driven by Robert Lister, an eager undergraduate student who was paid thirty-five cents an hour for the task but willingly would have cut classes and worked for nothing just to share in this adventure. He and a fraternity brother climbed into the cab ready to join the convoy to Albuquerque. Off to archaeological immortality! Lister turned on the ignition, revved the motor, and the obstinate vehicle did not move. He tried again. Same results. Somewhat embarrassed in front of his superiors (who, after all, were already graduate students) he got out to inspect. What he saw was the front wheels entirely off the ground. They had been lifted by the weight in the trunk bed of an encapsulated, eighteen-foot long slab of wall estimated at some four thousand pounds. Obviously, what was absent was traction.

To remedy this unforeseen predicament, the young men hastened to the local farm supply store in Bernalillo, purchased burlap feed bags, hiked to the sand bars by the river, and filled them. Then with great effort and sweat, they carried them one by one to the incapacitated truck and dumped them on fenders and cab. Slowly the front end descended, putting tires on soil and making movement possible. Three trucks carrying priceless booty from the distant past made their way down back roads of the valley and up to the barren, wind-swept mesa above Albuquerque, where in the 1930s the groupings of university buildings sat in relative isolation as a beacon of learning.

What these students of Pueblo archaeology were to learn was that scholarly inspection of what their ponderous concretions of plaster, cloth, and wood contained was going to be a nerve-wracking retreat backward in time from uppermost to innermost, almost transparent, skims of plaster, and that task would consume two years.

Funded by the Works Progress Administration (WPA), the laboratory crew included, in addition to Vivian and Bliss, the Frank Palmers, Vance Davis, Robert Lister, an individual named Hawker, and the Plains Indian artist Paul Goodbear (Figs. 21, 22). Marjorie Tichy (Lambert) (Fig. 23), then an instructor at the university, was responsible for obtaining the necessary materials for the delicate task of removing the murals from their protective cocoons and recording them. Her purchase orders reflect the financial hard times of the 1930s as she requested as much ambroid and ambroid solvent as could be sent at a price not to exceed eight dollars or whatever amount of plasticine she could get for three dollars.[8] Her other purchases were for art pigments, sable art brushes, light adobe oil paint, 50-inch artists' canvas, palette knives, alcohol, Duco cement, wall sealer, lamp black, turpentine, linseed oil, celotex cardboard, 20-gauge galvanized wire, pulverized papier mache, and cold-water glue. Her orders also included acacia powder, the source for the gum arabic used as a medium for watercolor painting. Then work began.

Fig. 21.
Laboratory crew
of Kuaua mural
project. Left to
right: Hacker,
Vance Davis,
Mrs. Frank Palmer,
Frank Palmer,
Wesley Bliss.

Fig. 22. Student laboratory crew assigned
to the Kuaua mural project. Left to right:
Vance Davis, Robert Lister, Paul Goodbear.

Fig. 23. Marjorie Tichy Lambert at
right, 1935.

Maintaining a humid atmosphere to prevent the plaster from drying too rapidly, the team removed the front wood frame and plaster-of-paris. Getting at the paintings was a far more demanding task than Bliss's previous experience with releasing bones from plaster shells. Wielding flexible palette knives, the workers slowly and painstakingly scrutinized each successive layer as they worked inward. They meticulously scraped sterile surfaces. If there was a hint of additional original treatment, the neophyte technicians made notes, took photographs, and did drawings. Some of the copies were full four-and-a-half foot size; others were smaller reproductions on canvas that could be more easily handled for study. In both instances, great care was taken to make the work accurate as to color and relative dimensions. These copies proved useful in clarifying the depictions because they eliminated the distracting background crazing of the plaster surfaces and splotchy soil discolorations. Ultimately the original wall paintings were tediously transferred to an adobe-coated pressboard backing through several treatments of solvents and a cloth covering to which, if all went well, the portrayals would adhere. As a final step attended by much tension for the workers, they slowly pulled away the cloth, hopefully leaving the intact paintings behind on the pressboard.[9] The workers were satisfied that one by one the Kuaua murals were secured for posterity. Bliss must have been blissful and doubtless relieved.

The plaster composite consisted of eighty-seven distinguishable layers. Twenty of them, or a little less than one-fourth, carried designs. Others were slightly splotched with red or black pigment that had disintegrated into nothing. Perhaps these surfaces had been destroyed or damaged before washes were painted over them. As the murals emerged like ghosts from the grave, it was apparent that everything portrayed on the walls of Kiva III was derived from the native ideology. Narrative or historical painting was not in evidence. The missing Franciscans were still missing. Like others before and after him, Villagrá may have spiced up his report to impress officialdom. What better way than to show the heathens slaughtering the most noble of men, the teachers of truth as the Spaniards saw it.

By the 1300s when Kuaua was first settled in the houses along the south side of the community, which the diggers called the Lummis unit, the people had the skills and biases leading to the blooming of mural art. Customarily they had plastered their walls with liquefied adobe mud. Sometimes they had painted them with solid dados or random geometric or naturalistic elements, using colorants formulated from mineral and vegetal sources. Add that background to an ageless tradition of visual expression of inner beliefs, such as shown in petroglyphs and pictographs, and it was a logical step to turn walls into iconographic billboards under the stimulus of a new religious vitality. Anthropologists judge that religion to have been the katsina cult.

The Kuaua artists turned to their natural worlds to put their thoughts into graphic form: themselves, their equipment for an agricultural mode of life, the flora, fauna, and physical landscape around them, and varied imagery of anthropomorphic and zoomorphic combinations. But all these motifs were manikins or backdrops enriched by coloration, ornamentation, or accessories that had particular supernatural meanings to painters and native viewers. It was an esoteric vocabulary generally unintelligible to the uninitiated and likely varied in small details from village to village, and it was constantly changing. The sterile layers were either periodic housekeeping or served to decisively conclude a particular rite.

Among elements taken from the local environment were depictions of fish. What was more expectable with a perennial river, doubtless with a piscine population, out the front door? It surely is not puzzling that in the other three localities with excavated murals (to be discussed later), all in generally waterless terrain, fish are almost absent in wall paintings. Another environmentally related motif is an accurate portrayal of a bison (Fig. 24). It hints at some nearby presence of these animals, if not immediate then no farther than a day's walk eastward to where the great interior plains of North America begin. As confirmation of the occasional use of these mammals, some bones unearthed at neighboring Puaray were tentatively identified as those of bison.[10] Ceramic jars with tapered bottoms and what seem to be depictions of fringed leggings likewise hint at exchange with Plains Indians.

Fig. 24. Black bison figure spitting water droplets.

It was the sad history of early Southwestern archaeology that some participants in the discipline found excavation far more entertaining than analysis and reporting the results. Many specimens and notes were lost over the years as work went unpublished. In the case of Kuaua, the disruptions of World War II, the dispersal of those who had worked on the project, and other professional commitments delayed detailed publication of any study of the murals or other features of the site. No technical report on the archaeology or artifacts ever was written. Thirty years

Fig. 25. Bertha Dutton.

passed before a report on the murals was prepared. This was the work of Bertha Dutton (Fig. 25), once a student on the dig and later curator of ethnology of the Museum of New Mexico, where the murals were permanently housed.[11] By the time she turned to this effort, regional scholars were concerning themselves with socioreligious aspects of prehistoric life that could be ascertained through archaeology. Consequently Dutton sought to interpret the symbolic meaning of the images rather than their aesthetic or fabricated qualities.

To get Native American perspectives, Dutton needed help from someone knowledgeable in katsina lore. She ruled out trying to find an informant at Sandia Pueblo, the sole modern Tiwa town in the nearby vicinity, because the last known katsina ceremony held there was in 1660.[12] She also considered Keresan villages just to the north as being unlikely places to find elders willing to talk about sacred matters. Those groups continued the katsina rituals but had a reputation for being very secretive about them. Nevertheless, she turned to a Keres friend at Laguna Pueblo. He either did not recognize many of the Kuaua illustrations or was reticent to discuss them. Ultimately he died before passing on much information. Finally a Zuni ceremonial leader agreed to cooperate. Over a period of many months, he perused the reproductions and conveyed his impressions of them. Meanwhile, Dutton plunged into studies of Pueblo religion and mythology.

In her book *Sun Father's Way* Dutton described the painted motifs layer by layer and her informant's conclusions about them. This makes for interesting reading but must be treated cautiously as the ideas of one individual from a different time and place.

One of the most complete panels was on the fifty-sixth layer, counting out from the innermost, or earliest, layer. Dutton identified this as the Great Corn Drama.[13] Six figures stand between tall, stylized corn stalks to which cobs with silk are attached. Based on information from her informant, the personages are said to be a god of music, Nighttime Woman, Fire Man, Yellow Corn Maiden, Lightning Man, and Universal Deity: Corn (Earth) Mother and Sky (Sun) Father. Five of them are drawn in frontal position but with legs and feet in profile and give the impression of having come out of the same mold. They are stiff and lack expression. Some wear what must be strands of beads, such as have been recovered archaeologically as long, open-end ropes, wrapped many times around necks and looped down over chests (Fig. 26). The symbolic identities of these personages are recognized by the articles they carry and some garment details, such as position or number of tassels on sashes. The masked Universal Deity is unique in the entire collection (Fig. 27). She wears a flared dresslike costume instead of the usual kilt or blanket-dress and carries a quiver in one hand and two rods in the other. According to some observers, every line, color, or minute feature on or about her refers to something in the Pueblo mythical cosmology. However, analogy of these details with present-day ritual remains uncertain. Furthermore, those who are not part of the culture risk reading too much into the record.

*Fig. 26. Two figures from a scene believed to depict a ceremony for fertiliza-
tion. The human on the left, wearing typical black kilt and bead necklace
with shell pendant, holds a hoop through which a pointed-bottom jar spills
water. The two-toned individual on the right is said to be a dual personage.*

A quadruped, for example, may be a recognizable and readily depicted
part of the environment having no esoteric meaning.

A second special panel was that on the sixty-first layer. Dutton calls
it the Depiction of the Universe and interprets it as showing weather
control and hunting and planting activities being carried out by three
deities. They are drawn face forward and are separated by birds, a fish, a
serpent, spilling water, zigzag lightning bolts, jars, and other lesser items.
Colors used are black, white, yellow, and earth-red against a light tan
plaster made from a mixture of silt and adobe.[14]

Two prone figures wearing exaggerated fish masks were on the uppermost layer of the wall on either side of a small niche. They are identified

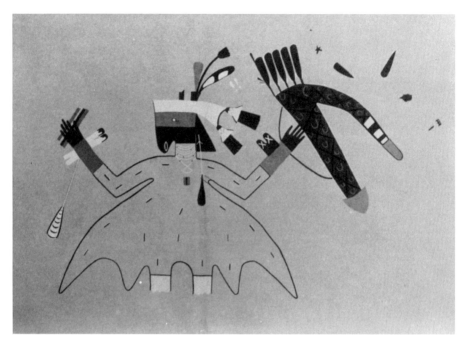

Fig. 27. Female figure identified as the Universal Deity. Colors are white, yellow, earth-red, and black.

as the sons of the Sun (Fig. 28). A terraced motif topping the niche may have been an altar symbol. Excavators found a stone pipe, a projectile point, and some turquoise and other stones in the niche. Perhaps these objects composed an offering.

Dutton correlated other scenes with initiation procedures and seasonal hunting, blessing, solstice, and scalp ceremonies, some of which related to the curing and warrior societies. By extension, she attempted to interpret propitious or troubled times for the inhabitants. She became convinced that the cultural infusion stimulating these graphic works, first suspected from the appearance of rectangular kivas in round kiva territory, came from the west or southwest, that is, Western Pueblos (Hopi and Zuni) or Mogollon tribes. This reflects a Zuni interpretation. She listed a complex of diffused traits that included red pottery with decora-

Fig. 28. A pair of horizontal figures wearing elongated masks or headpieces have been interpreted as sons of the Sun. Colors are yellow, earth-red, white, and black.

tive patterns in a mineral pigment that vitrified upon being fired and, more important to the context being considered here, a philosophical reorientation that embodied societal groupings, obligations, and manifest aesthetic expressions such as wall paintings in kivas as part of certain rituals. With the latter, the katsina cult had come to Kuaua.

Scholars define the katsina cult as one devoted to a multitude of spirits who serve as intermediaries between the people and the deities. Primarily they are rainmakers who bring the blessings of rejuvenation and life to an arid land. This is underscored in the Kuaua murals by almost half of the individual motifs being identified with water or phenomena related to weather.[15] These motifs are showers of dots representing rain or spilling water, clouds, rainbows, and lightning. It is not surprising that the katsinas also are associated with fertility and curing. The katsinas are represented graphically through wall paintings and dramatically through rites in the secrecy of kivas, and they are impersonated by masked dancers singing sacred chants in the public plazas within settlement compounds. The cult evolved around this set of traits, in which all members of a group participated, and bonded together what otherwise might have been disparate Pueblo entities coming together in the late thirteenth and through the fourteenth centuries as a consequence of displacements due to environmental or other circumstances.

Most students of the subject believe the ultimate source for this cult was Mexico, even though its practices actually were a mix of indigenous and borrowed traits. The routes and specific times by which most of its basic attributes reached the Pueblo world on the Colorado Plateau are uncertain. One path may have been north from the Chihuahua region along the Rio Grande valley. Polly and Curtis Schaafsma feel that the Jornada Mogollon in the lower Rio Grande district introduced the katsina cult to the middle Rio Grande, along with some Mexican design motifs such as masks, cloud terraces, and horned snakes.[16] Another diffusion route may have been northward through central Arizona. Adams suggests a first introduction to Kuaua from Hopi about 1400 and a second overlay of traits from the Jornada Mogollon after 1450.[17] Some persons argue for an indigenous source. Whatever the background was, by some time in the mid 1400s katsinas were a customary part of Kuaua life. The cult was still functioning when Coronado and his troops reached the area. However, so few Spanish artifacts were recovered at Kuaua that Dutton concluded that the place already was being deserted.[18] Excavators were unable to find any datable wood samples that could confirm this idea. Coronado may not have slept at Kuaua either.

Or did he? Study has identified sherds incorporated in the Kiva III altar construction as dating to the 1600 to 1630 period. Dutton and Tichy also noted the presence at the site of a type of glaze-decorated pottery ware that archaeologists think representative of the second half of the seventeenth century.[19] It is possible that the wall paintings predate the various periodic refurbishings of the altar, but this pottery in it implies that the kiva was in use well into the time of the Spanish occupation of New Mexico. Inasmuch as no Catholic mission was placed at Kuaua and presumably no priest was in residence there, the inhabitants may have continued observing their calendric katsina rituals geared to seasonal changes without outside interference. Or, the seven plain coats of plaster covering the last decorated one might mean that the kiva society at some time had ceased its katsina practices but continued to use the chamber for other purposes.

A second rectangular kiva in the northeast corner of Kuaua likewise had been embellished with wall paintings. They were barely recognizable and beyond recapture but impressed observers as probably being a late echo of what had gone before in Kiva III. Perhaps they were executed in Spanish times.

Continuing his all-out pursuit of Coronado, Hewett sent an exploratory party to Paako at the same time digs were underway at Kuaua. Paako was a contemporaneous site on the eastern side of the Sandia Mountains but occupied by a different linguistic group. Archaeologists found a square kiva in a houseblock there that had evidence that the walls once were covered with paintings.[20] All that remained were bits of scaling plaster containing traces of earth-red, black, white, and yellow colors. Diggers could not reclaim anything. The find was important, nonetheless, in showing that the katsina cult had spread east beyond the Tiguex province. At least that was the inference the researchers drew from some signs of polychromatic painting. Although Paako must have been known to the Spaniards, diggers did not recover any of their artifacts. Again, no Coronado.

On March 7, 1935, New Mexico designated Kuaua as a state monument. Three years later Hewett secured government support through the Works Progress Administration and the National Youth Administration (NYA) to clear most of the community. From time to time as many as seventy local men were engaged in this massive effort under the direction of Albert Ely, another of Hewett's advanced students. It was disappointing to them that they found no further painted kivas. The absence of such religious embellishments in two other coeval excavated kivas and several domestic rooms that appeared to have been converted into kivas might be explained by natural causes that had eradicated the evidence, the failure of diggers to identify multilayered plaster as being decorated, or the cult's simply having failed to gain a strong toehold at Kuaua.

One thrust of the final work at Kuaua was the rebuilding of the destroyed Kiva III. The modern masons laid up over a hundred thousand molded adobe bricks rather than the hardened balls used by the ancients. They roofed the kiva and provided it with a smoke hole and entry ladder such as once existed. Native American artists painted on two walls copies of the forty-first original layer.[21] That layer actually was the forty-sixth plaster coat down from the surface and was identifiable only on the north and west walls of the ancient chamber. Figures reproduced include a duck or goose spraying water. Also present is an anthropomorph with a masked face; a white, earth-red, and black feather headdress; an elongated horizontal body with one human leg; an orange, earth-red, and black wing; and black and white tail feathers. A standing humanlike figure in black, a second frontal personage garbed in black with a broad tasseled white sash, a partial yellow deer with white rump, and a stalk of black corn round out the display. When work was completed, visitors could descend into the kiva, where its dark enclosure and painted walls heighten the sense of sacredness that once pervaded this sanctuary.

Before the Kuaua project terminated, Ely found himself in trouble. In hiring his crew, he had sworn that all men were citizens of the United States as required by the WPA regulations. A Bernalillo grocer, Ignacio Valdes, filed a complaint with Bliss, general overseer of the work, that three of the diggers were in the country illegally and that he would report them and the university unless these delinquents paid their overdue food bills.[22] The outcome of this affair is not known, but even though Ely might have been unaware of the true nationality of these laborers, he probably was reprimanded and the noncitizens deported to Mexico. This incident does show that sixty years have not seen much change in the ebb and flow of labor forces in and out of border states.

The following year builders erected a spacious museum of Pueblo Revival style designed by New Mexico's premier architect at the time, John Gaw Meem. Natural materials and handwork made it blend into its setting at the east side of the ruin overlooking the Rio Grande, a pleasant vista that has not changed appreciably since Kuaua was a flourishing town. One wing of the building accommodates a display under glass of fourteen of the rescued wall paintings. They are so darkened and deteriorated that it is almost impossible to make out the features. Fortunately, small drawings beside each panel explain the contents.

Exhibits in the center room of the museum tell the story of the coming of the Spaniards, who in essence have never left. The majority population of Sandoval County, in which this monument is located, remains Native American, but the county seat of Bernalillo is Hispanic. A much diluted non-Indian authority continues. As a nod to Coronado, although he may have just passed through, the facility became the Coronado State Monument just in time for the Coronado Cuarto Centennial. Hewett's goal was achieved in spirit. The facility was dedicated in May 1940 with a number of state and local officials attending. One can assume that no Native American leaders were invited, for what did they have to celebrate? That night a Coronado pageant was held at the University of New Mexico stadium. It included enactment of the conquistadors' entrada performed by a cast of hundreds of local people, many of whom could trace their Hispanic family ties back to that historic event.

The present status of the murals recalls the bromide about a medical operation being successful, but the patient dies. Archaeologists recovered the wall paintings and through them embarked on an unending quest for understanding Pueblo thought as demonstrated through this medium. The 1930s laboratory crew undertook a technical task for which they had no guidelines. The images upon which they spent so much time and effort now are so faint and faded as to be undecipherable. Some kind of surface preservative might have lessened this disintegration. Both the full-size and the smaller, one-half and one-third size, reproductions on canvas are so brittle that they can be unfurled only with extreme care. Had curators stored them flat instead of rolled that problem might have been avoided. Belated conservation using modern materials and techniques awaits a substantial investment in talent and money, an effort just now being initiated. The only publication dealing in depth with the murals, that by Dutton, is long out of print. The plates used to produce its colored illustrations unaccountably were destroyed. The sole remaining usable resource are several folders of black and white photographic prints of the reproductions. These circumstances make the rebuilt kiva in the south plaza of Kuaua especially valuable. In their protected environment, the paintings copied from those on Layer 41 continue to provide thoughtful viewers a tiny insight into the psyche and artistic skills of the Pueblo people. Meanwhile, the adobe walls of the town around slowly return to the earth from which they arose. Across the highway to the south, the sixteenth- and seventeenth-century settlement of

Puaray has become a pockmarked gravel pit, reputedly thanks to the county highway department.

With today's hypersensitivity to ethnic issues, it is probable that were the Kuaua wall paintings found now, they would not be excavated. The scientists who carried out this 1930s project felt they were doing a service in adding to the pool of knowledge about the ancestral Pueblos in all its ramifications. Nonetheless, the people of Sandia Pueblo just ten miles away, who regard Kuaua as one of their ancestral homes, undoubtedly would protest at having sacred materials unearthed, photographed, drawn, published, and exhibited. They would think it as much a violation as the unearthing of 600 burials at this site and another 450 at Puaray, none of which have ever been scientifically examined beyond body orientation in graves.[23] Katsina rituals are still practiced in most of the Eastern Pueblos but not in Sandia Pueblo. That, however, is not apt to negate the Sandia people's objections. In fact, now out of respect for their wishes, visitors cannot photograph the paintings. The ticklish question of how deeply scientists should delve is one unlikely ever to be answered to the satisfaction of all parties.

Notes

1. Tichy, 1939, 151–154.

2. Bliss letter to Gordon Vivian, September 1, 1959 (Archives, Laboratory of Anthropology/Museum of Indian Art and Culture, Santa Fe, New Mexico).

3. G. Vivian, 1935, 113.

4. Bliss, 1948, 218–219; Hewett, 1938, 23.

5. Dutton, 1962, 180, Pl. XXV, Layer A-8.

6. Stout and Gettens, 1932, 3–8.

7. Dutton, 1962, 27–33; G. Vivian, 1935, 113–119.

8. Tichy letter to Ambroid Company, Brooklyn, New York, June 16, 1936 (Archives, Laboratory of Anthropology/Museum of Indian Art and Culture, Santa Fe, New Mexico).

9. Bliss, 1936, 81–87; Bliss 1948, 218–223, Pls. XXI–XXII.

10. Tichy, 1939, 160.

11. Dutton, 1962.

12. E. C. Adams, 1991, 19.

13. Dutton, 1962, 101–121, Pl. XIV.

14. Ibid., 122–123, Pls. XV, XVI.

15. Crotty, 1995, 362.

16. Schaafsma and Schaafsma, 1974, 535–545.

17. E. C. Adams, 1991, 120, 186.

18. Dutton, 1962, 32–33.

19. Ibid., 23, 32; Tichy, 1938, 71–79.

20. Tichy, 1938, 71–79.

21. Dutton, 1962, 34, Pl. VIII.

22. Bliss note to Albert Ely, September 30, 1938 (Archives, Laboratory of Anthropology/Museum of Indian Art and Culture, Santa Fe, New Mexico).

23. Luhrs and Ely, 1939, 27–32.

Off the Wall in Jeddito

Although the Hopi Indians have adopted a thin veneer of mainstream Americana, they have retained more of their traditional culture than other Pueblo groups. Legend has it that exactly three hundred years ago they stormed their primary easternmost community, killed the Catholic priests and their own blood brothers, tore asunder walls, and left behind a smoldering heap of devastation. This cataclysm occurred because, whether from spinelessness or conviction, the residents had allowed the Franciscans to reestablish themselves there in the wake of the Pueblo Revolt of 1680–1692. The town was Awatovi, the place where the tide of Spanish influence was turned back from Hopiland forever because the Hopi were willing to destroy their own in order to destroy outsiders.

In 1935 the Peabody Museum of Harvard University launched what was to become a five-season archaeological assault on Awatovi, in northeastern Arizona. This project was the continuation of a long pattern of eastern institutions' conducting prehistoric research in the Southwest. At the time when work began at Awatovi the site comprised several enormous rock-strewn mounds covering acres, potholes left from sunken semisubterranean kivas, open plazas, and the high skeleton walls of a mission church and compound that spread across the southern end of Antelope Mesa (Fig. 29).[1] It was the most prominent of five sizable communities along the eastern brink of the mesa, the others with the tongue-twisting names of Kawaika-a, Chakpahu, Ne Suftanga, Kokopnyama, and Lululongturqui. The tableland was covered with a sparse pinyon-juniper and scrub growth that provided little shade or protection from wind. Views of distant landmarks rimmed the horizon above a broad valley below the mesa. Through the valley ran the drainage bed of what was called the Jeddito River, although it actually channeled water only periodically in this arid land. The surrounding district has taken its name from this drainage.

The reconnaissance team set up a tent encampment near the ruins in a sandy swale. The accommodations included a cement-lined cistern for

Fig. 29. Ruined Awatovi hugs the tip of Antelope Mesa with distant views of the Jeddito valley.

Fig. 30. Awatovi field camp; wooden building was dining hall/kitchen.

Fig. 31. Hopi workers hauling water for camp cistern.

water hauled in wagons from a spring in a nearby valley and a generator that would bring a bit of modern civilization to an island in the wilderness of the fabled "Indian country" (Figs. 30, 31). Conduits for supplies were arranged with the operator of a regional trading post and a store in the Santa Fe Railroad whistle stop of Winslow, seventy tortuous miles to the south.[2]

As the project developed under the directorship of J. O. Brew, then a bright Harvard graduate student, specialists from many related disciplines became either permanent staff or visiting consultants. They included physiographer John Hack, geologist Kirk Bryan, ethnobotanist Volney Jones, ceramic technician Anna Shepard, architect Ross Montgomery, dendrochronologist Ned Hall, surveyor Robert Burgh, and photographers Edward Beckwith and García-Robion. Graduate students and assorted others with interest and willing hands also were part of the effort. Of course, most important were the leader, Brew, whose duty it was to keep everything on track, and a camp cook, Lindsay Thompson, who could turn out delicious meals under adverse conditions. The latter's morning griddle cakes became legendary.

A labor crew of young Hopi men was hired by Brew with funds supplied this time not by federal relief agencies, although the Great Depression still was a painful reality, but by three wealthy Harvard patrons. This, too, was a familiar pattern (Fig. 32). Equal numbers of individuals were recruited from First and Second Mesa, the two groups bunking in their own squad tents and eating separately. This struck the Anglo staff as strange — all of the laborers being Hopi — but such dichotomies based on village affiliation were part of their customary routines. They did work together on the excavations with seeming harmony. On weekends some climbed into a Dodge Commercial truck to drive the eight or so miles back to their homes (Fig. 33). Others preferred to trot the distance. On Monday mornings they repeated the return trip.

Camp life was troubled by summer heat, incessant wind, and blowing sand. To compensate, there were evening card games, music from a second-hand piano, occasional visits to native ceremonies, and childlike

Fig. 32. *Hopi crew at Awatovi camp. Anglos include J. O. Brew at far right; next to him, Charles Amsden and Watson Smith; other Anglos not identified.*

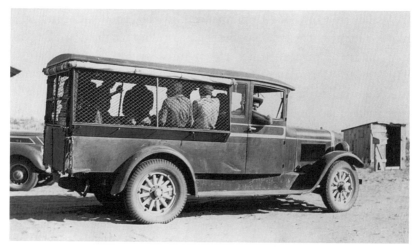

Fig. 33. *Dodge Commercial truck taking Hopi crew to their villages for the weekend. Lancaster in cab.*

romps down the numerous sand dunes that banked the mesa escarpments. Life under field conditions was further sweetened by association with persons having divergent backgrounds and interests and a group sense of doing something meaningful and extraordinary. The parade of colleagues who came to see what that was comprised a roster of the profession's notables at the time. A collegial atmosphere prevailed that brought to the camp individuals like Ted Kidder, Earl Morris, Jesse Nusbaum, Ted Sayles, Emil Haury, Charles Amsden, George Brainerd, Fred Eggan, and Douglas Scott to share ideas and just to rejoice in the pleasure of the paths they had chosen.

Young Brew could hardly have hoped for a more auspicious beginning for an archaeological career, this being only his second field endeavor. Personally he was rotund, jovial, in love with the expedition's secretary, and by Ivy League standards from the wrong side of the tracks. Professionally he proved to be an able manager and developed diplomatic skills in dealing with Native American leaders who controlled the land on which the ruin stood. Moreover, he had the good fortune of having three special crew members who made him look good. Their contributions were many, but none of them would have a place in today's highly competitive scene where an advanced degree is required for the lowliest field hand.

First, there was Al Lancaster, the soft-spoken, hard-as-nails farmer who had a few years earlier learned that for him digging in ruins was far more interesting than digging in his bean fields. He had the tactile skills that Brew lacked and competently directed the Hopi crews as if he had been doing it all his life. His antics and unpretentiousness made them his friends for life.

Then there was Hattie Cosgrove, wife of a small-town merchant-turned-archaeologist, Burton Cosgrove, who abruptly died soon after the Awatovi work began. Hattie stayed on to run the pottery lab and became an unofficial, gracious hostess for the many visitors. For years she had known that counting potsherds was more pleasurable for her than taking inventories of nuts and bolts in the family hardware store.

Fig. 34. In Awatovi camp. Left to right: Helen Claflin, Al Lancaster, Watson Smith, John Hack.

Finally, there was Watson Smith—scholarly, urbane, and so articulate that he believed one should not use a two syllable word if a six syllable one would do. It would be he who would put many of the results of the Awatovi expedition into polished prose because he felt that more challenging than writing legal briefs (Fig. 34).

There was an appeal to the Awatovi expedition beyond its scientific one. It was to be in a part of the West that in the 1930s still was little touched by what was going on in the rest of the nation. There was an aura of foreignness in the limitless sweeps of emptiness only spottily inhabited by Hopi and Navajo Indians who continued ageless traditional language, housing, dress, and ritual. These residents traveled in covered, horse-drawn, Studebaker wagons—the fabled prairie schooners—or on horseback, while just a few miles away other Americans whizzed along in cars speeding down Route 66.

Since the late nineteenth century the Hopi in particular had been the subject of many ethnographic studies. Their stony cubicles on rocky uplands, their women seated on the ground coiling vessels out of inert clay, their menfolk in bizarre masks and costumes dancing with snakes while gourds rattled and drums thumped, all were fodder for the Sunday newspaper supplements. Most prehistoric research that had been done to that time in the broader district concerned itself with times leading up to the actual appearance of an entity that could be called Hopi, not the early Hopi themselves. Much of that work had taken place in colorful, wondrous landscapes containing ruined cliff dwellings replete with artifacts and desiccated human remains, thus exotic materials to be fantasized as the "romance" of archaeology. Every man and woman in the Awatovi expedition would confess to whetted appetites for adventure in that setting denied to their desk-bound peers. They also would hasten to proclaim sincere desires to lift the curtain on the human drama that had been played out there.

The 1936 season had scarcely commenced when Lancaster spotted flecks of colored plaster in room fill. This was a clue to something exciting. He and Brew knew that early in the century an intriguing wall painting of a diving bird and a pair of human legs over a basal wave and dot border had been reported from the neighboring Jeddito site of Kawaika-a.[3] Just at the time of Lancaster's observations, Smith joined the expedition party. Since he had no assigned job, Brew put him in charge of overseeing what might develop from these tantalizing traces. He became the kiva mural man, little knowing that academic exercise would consume many years of his life.

It was a rare coincidence that two major mural discoveries had been made within several years of each other in the early to mid 1930s. Further, the murals were in different physical environments, of different styles, and dated to different periods in the Pueblo past. In the Mesa Verde province there was the geometric brown and white panel at Lowry Ruin dated to the very early twelfth century, and in the central Rio Grande valley there was the figural polychromatic Kuaua panels tentatively dated to the mid-fifteenth century. Now the possibility of still other murals adding to the range, variation, and life span of the art form of religious wall paintings was heady stuff. Search for kiva murals quickly became an important focus of the Awatovi expedition.

The first sighting of a painted panel at Awatovi was in Room 218, a small rectangular kiva in the West Mound. In a cross section of a loose piece of the wall Lancaster counted more than a hundred layers of plaster.[4] Subsequent analysis would reveal that only twenty-six of them, approximately one-fourth, bore painted designs, of which twenty-three were identifiable designs.[5] Still clinging to one layer under several others of brown adobe was a very fragmentary scrap of what had been a simple pattern of undetermined content executed in white, black, red, and yellow. It was not much other than a lure for further exploration.[6]

Over four field seasons excavators uncovered nine additional rectangular kivas at Awatovi and fifteen others at Kawaika-a bearing various numbers of wall paintings. Not all kivas had such decoration. In total there were twenty-five embellished walls. The chambers themselves were quite standardized, all rectangular at twelve to eighteen feet in length and seven-and-a-half to twelve feet in width. The chamber floors were flagstone, the walls were stone masonry or, more rarely, hand-modeled adobe brick, and the upper portions of the walls were either missing or badly deteriorated.

Some walls had been prepared for painted decoration by being coated with a clay and quartz sand mortar into which were embedded strips of woven matting or horizontally or vertically laid grass and reeds. A final, fine-grained, brownish-red plaster was the finish coat. It had been smoothed by hand, by a flat rock or board, or by a piece of chamois. This kind of meticulous preliminary work was necessitated by the inherent irregular surfaces of stone masonry as opposed to the flatter faces of Kuaua adobe walls.

Locally obtained mineral pigments dissolved in water, to which some kind of binder or vehicle such as animal oil may have been added, produced twelve color variations.[7] These were yellow, red, and orange from iron oxide; pink and vermilion from red ochre and white clay; salmon; brown from red ochre and charcoal; purple; blue from azurite; green from malachite; white from kaolin; and gray from clay. Only black came from an organic source, probably charcoal. These paints were applied over dry plaster, hence rode on the surface rather than being absorbed by a wet background as in the case of true fresco. Painting was done with a brush of one or several yucca fibers, a feather, a folded cornhusk, or fingertips. Of course, brushes of pigs' bristle, such as were used in Europe, were unknown before the arrival of the Spaniards.

One kiva was completely intact and had a special significance in the seventeenth-century history of Awatovi. The Franciscan friars who came to the settlement in 1629 to establish a mission and bring these pagans into the fold of Christianity had seen fit to erect their church directly over the kiva, a first church foundation elsewhere having been abandoned. Diggers clearing the high altar in the nave and the adjoining sanctuary probed beneath them about three feet to encounter preserved roof beams in place.[8] Upon removal of the beams, the workmen saw that the kiva below had been filled with clean sand, of which there was an abundance over the mesa top and sides, leaving all the interior features undisturbed and the painted walls untouched. The Awatovians coerced into doing this arduous job would not have found it traumatic. They themselves customarily dumped domestic trash into vacated kivas. The fact that these rooms once had been special sanctuaries had no enduring significance for them.

Smith felt that the kiva beneath the altar, Room 788 in the records, probably had been in use when the padres selected that portion of the community as the location for their church.[9] Undoubtedly it was a newly functioning facility when Pedro de Tovar, on assignment from Coronado to explore west of Hawikuh (Zuni), came through Hopiland in 1540. The kiva walls that were still aglow with vivid images when the diggers discovered them might well have been covered over with a thin wash at the end of rites enacted before them. We will never know if the clerics stopped those rites in progress, but they did follow the practice of superposition, common in the conquest and conversion eras, to demonstrate the superiority of their religion over that of the unenlightened native peoples. Curiously, in their accounts to church authorities they made no mention of these painted walls that might have justified their perceived need to initiate such action. It was just taken for granted.

It is ironic that what the padres hid in this instance and the motivations for its embellishments survived the ravages of time far better here than did their own edifices and their teachings. Moreover, their placement of the church on top of a kiva probably did not have the impact the priests intended. Superpositioning of one structure over an earlier one was an age-old pattern with the Pueblos. They regarded a village as an organism that was dying and growing simultaneously: from the earth, back to the earth, next door or on top did not matter. At Awatovi there were examples of several stories of dwelling rooms built over earlier kivas.[10] The clerics dictated the style of the ecclesiastical compound. It was diferent in scale and configuration from anything the Indians had known previously, but the materials and workmanship were familiar. The services that went on inside those buildings differed from their own but nevertheless were aimed at invisible spirits or beings. Further, even though this one kiva may have been obliterated as an example, katsina believers surely continued their affairs in secret for three-quarters of a century, because once the Spaniards were expelled, the cult openly flourished again in other Hopi towns, including four that once had Catholic missions.

Having no experience in this sort of endeavor and at a loss as to how to proceed, Smith sought help from Vivian and Bliss. They came to Awatovi to share the knowledge they had gained from the Kuaua mural project. Smith found some ideas on procedures to be useful, but the field circumstances and the condition and volume of the paintings were sufficiently different from those at Kuaua to make it imperative that he find other solutions. Obviously, neither time, money, nor mere practicality would allow the crew to jacket and remove entire walls, cart them over the two sandy ruts across the Hopi and Navajo reservations that sufficed for roads, and put them in a Santa Fe freight car bound for Boston and the Peabody, where there was inadequate storage or laboratory space for what would have been enormous tonnage. Work of recording and

Fig. 35. *Cleaning and recording Awatovi kiva wall paintings. Left to right: Hattie Cosgrove, Watson Smith, Mrs. Donald Scott.*

stripping the panels sequentially had to be done in the field. Remounting and reproduction then could be carried out back at Cambridge.[11]

The first step in dealing with the wall paintings was to expose them. Smith reversed the usual excavation techniques of working down wall surfaces to floor level in order to define the unit and then clearing out deposition in the room center. Believing that the weight of the fill was necessary to hold plaster of uncertain durability in place, he had laborers first plug the room center to floor level and then slowly clear the fill toward the walls, hoping to avoid sudden changes in pressure and atmosphere.

The brilliant sunlight of a cloudless summertime Arizona sky created such glare bouncing off some walls that occasionally it was necessary to install temporary roofing over work areas (Fig. 35). The original roofs had long since disappeared. In one instance at the kiva beneath the church, roofing was constructed to keep workers warm as they strove to finish a job before snowfall. Although the original roof beams were found in place, the materials covering them were gone. The beams themselves had been removed to facilitate excavation. Discovered late in the 1938 season, this kiva promised to yield some of the finest, most detailed of all the murals. Smith could not leave them exposed over the winter, so he and several helpers remained in camp working as rapidly as circumstances permitted until the end of November. By that time nighttime temperatures were dipping near zero, making sitting in the kiva depression and trying to draw with stiff fingers an intolerable experience. In order to continue their task, the men erected a plank roof over the site and outfitted it with a central hatchway for entry and glass panes for light. They lowered an empty oil drum down to a masonry bench at one end of the room, turned it on its side, and used it as a stove. The kiva was once again as cozy as when the old Awatovians were busy at their looms, painting the walls, or performing for their gods.

Each phase of the recording and removal of the paintings was fraught with the danger of damaging them and required repeated experimentation with techniques and materials. Smith tackled these challenges with gusto, often with the help of wives of the various visitors or hired hands. Penrose Davis (Penny Worman) was one of the latter (Fig. 36). At the outset Smith and his troop of volunteers patched cracks in the plaster layers using a deposit of calcareous material and fine quartz sand they found on the mesa.[12] They ground the mixture on a metate just as the artisans must have done centuries ago. They moistened the mixture with water and applied it by hand, or in some cases used a small grease gun to insert it under weak spots. When the patches dried, the bond was adequate without discoloration.

Layer by layer the team went from latest to earliest, tediously seeking cleavage lines in order to separate away sterile layers with scalpels and reach decorated ones. Actually Smith reported that the Boy Scout knife was the most useful tool, not too sharp nor too dull.[13] Occasional frameworks were put up against walls to help in photographing and copying. Most image-bearing layers exhibited mere plaster sherds, bits and pieces of what had been larger renditions. Workers cleaned all surfaces, photo-

Fig. 36. Artist Penny Davis, assistant
to Watson Smith, in Awatovi camp,
1939.

graphed them, and drew them to scale using a string grid hung over the
walls and gridded paper. It was slow work because the cracked, stained,
and worn surfaces made identification difficult and photographs rather
unsatisfactory. Drawings that eliminated the background problems were
more revealing. Black pencils were used for the outline copying. Colors
were precisely defined with reference to a standard color dictionary and
indicated on the field drawings by symbols. Such arbitrary selection inevitably posed ethical considerations for the researchers, but in the end
practicalities had to prevail. The methods generally were satisfactory because the original artists had painted solid zones of color without shad-
ing and outlined them in black. Smith saved paint samples for future
chemical analysis. Not all designs were stripped from the walls and

saved. Many were too fragile. The best-preserved, distinctive ones with possible symbolism were selected for this process. Of 178 designs, only 14 were kept for ultimate remounting and analysis.[14]

After experimenting with fifteen types of adhesive solutions to determine their viscosity, rates of evaporation, and flexibility, Smith selected one. Then he painted it over the design under scrutiny and patted overlapping squares of coarse muslin cloth on its surface. Next he applied a stripping solution and finally peeled the muslin mosaic away from the wall, taking the plaster layer with it. Timing was everything at each stage to ensure just the right degree of dryness. The muslin sheets were separated by newspaper and were stacked flat or rolled for shipment back to the Peabody Museum. Their analysis would take years.

The Jeddito tradition of kiva imagery came to an end with the arrival of the Franciscans. However, for their own purposes those clergymen tapped into what they must have hoped was native painting expertise. Bringing glazed tiles two thousand miles from workshops in central Mexico was out of the question. So the Franciscans, like other missionaries along the northern borderlands of empire, prevailed upon their neophytes to paint copies of the tiles for a wainscoting in the church nave and sacristy. Even though the priests surely were familiar with the true fresco technique as used in Europe, it appears that this painting was over dry rather than wet plaster. Any sort of decoration could have been used for the wainscoting. Nonetheless, the mindset of the priests was such that a place of worship, no matter how humble and far out on the peripheries of European culture, should have tile, if not the real thing then a reasonable facsimile.

At the time the church of San Bernardo de Aguatubi was being constructed at Awatovi, tile production was in high gear in Puebla in central Mexico. Because the tiles were formed in molds, they were of uniform size, shape, and thickness with straight edges. After being bisque fired, they were dipped in a lead glaze solution made white and opaque by the addition of a bit of tin oxide. This was the maiolica technique known in Spain for centuries. When air dry, each tile was painted with mineral pigments that would fire into a wide range of colors. Guild masters chose

*Fig. 37. Painted imitations of maiolica tiles on walls of San Bernardo de
Aguatubi sanctuary. The obviously fragile condition of the plaster prevented
preservation. Colors were black and orange on tan background.*

patterns for a particular production run, and each individual potter
in the workshop copied that pattern freehand. This meant that there
was minor variation from tile to tile. It was mass production on a pre-
industrial level.

Some tiles were meant to be used as friezes of running patterns. Others were installed together in groups, usually four to twelve to form a design. Most common were those tiles with a complete motif within itself
that could be used individually, contiguously, or alternating with comparable tiles.

The Awatovi priests chose the latter style of individual tiles as being
the most practical for their needs (Fig. 37). Above low painted dados of
solid colors, the Indian workers copied motifs of a geometric or floral na-

ture, such as rosettes or stripes.[15] Their draftsmanship was inferior to that of the kiva painters. This suggests that they did not understand their task, had little experience in the craft, or were bored with what must have seemed an endless repetition that was foreign to their thinking. They had no concept of preplanning an entire wall to ensure that all tiles would fit neatly into straight rows or a given space. The tilelike units were irregular in size and shape, and the designs were applied with greater abandon than that shown by the Spanish potters and were, in fact, quite appealing because of that. Moreover, the finished work appeared drab because it lacked the gloss and brilliance of glazed tile. One can guess that the priests resigned themselves to what they thought was the best that could be expected on this desolate frontier; they had made a token effort to have their establishment "proper." Besides, the decorative process kept the converts busy in the church, not only on the original endeavor but on repeated refurbishings through the years. At least twenty-one layers of plaster were evident in the nave. As in the case of the kivas, some layers were undecorated.

The three altars also were painted (Fig. 38). Instead of pseudo-tile motifs, what appear to have been imitations of tapestry and wrought iron tracery were executed with a great deal more skill.[16] Perhaps this was the work of one of the priests. Excavators also noted faded maroon or orange dados in the living quarters.

Smith studied the mission wall paintings in the course of excavation. With the exception of one altar face, they all were fragmentary, spotty, and in poor condition. He was unable to remove any of them. They were left to melt away. Later reproductions based upon field notes were made at the Peabody.

At the end of the 1939 season the Awatovi expedition ended. Political disputes among Hopi clans over territorial rights at Awatovi caused the Bureau of Indian Affairs not to renew the excavation permit. Brew had planned much further exploration of this site, as well as more survey and excavation in the entire Jeddito district.[17] Some thirteen hundred rooms of an estimated five thousand had been cleared, primarily in the

Fig. 38. Nave of 1629 San Bernardo de Aguatubi church with painted altar. The painted kiva was directly beneath the floor in the foreground, 1939.

West Mound, found to contain the earliest occupation dated to the late 1200s or early 1300s, and in the cluster of dwellings around and including the seventeenth-century mission complex. Sixty-five tests were made in other sectors of the settlement, presumably of intermediate ages, that were to be explored in greater detail at a future date. With these two primary site components and what reconnaissance and complete or partial excavation of twenty-one small sites in the surrounding region indicated, it seemed that the Jeddito had been Pueblo homeland for a thousand years.

The abrupt cessation of the proposed future inquiries into this continuum left the kiva mural aspects of the site, a monograph on pottery, and the later mission as the outstanding contributions of the Peabody

Museum staff to knowledge of the regional prehistoric and Spanish colonial periods. Brew, apparently because he felt that the Awatovi project was not satisfactorily completed, failed to write a comprehensive report on the work accomplished. This was lamentable because valuable data were not shared with the archaeological community about a settlement that was pivotal in terms of size, length and time of occupation, and geographical location. The opportunity for scientific study of a place of comparable importance is not likely to present itself again.

For the next two years at the Peabody Museum, Smith grappled with problems of remounting and reproducing the recovered Awatovi murals. His assistant was artist Penny Davis, who had been at Awatovi during the 1939 season. For them both it was another prolonged episode of trial and error, but this time they had the benefit of advice from conservators at Boston's many galleries. The panels of masonite Smith chose for backing were sized with glue on their reverse sides and were framed to prevent warping. He had brought original plaster from Awatovi that was washed, mixed with glue, and then spread over obverses of the panels, taking care not to make the coating too smooth so as to better emulate the original surfaces. Next the rolls or sheets of muslin stripping taken from the field and found to have remained flexible were carefully spread over this background. When this was dry, a laboratory technician used a paint spray gun and air compressor to cover the muslin and its protective plastic coating with a solvent. At the proper moment of absorption, he pulled the muslin away. The exposed paintings were sprayed once more with a mixture of formaldehyde and alcohol in order to harden their surfaces. It had been a long, expensive journey from the Awatovi kivas on Antelope Mesa across the continent to reach final rest in the Peabody basement.

For study and display purposes it was necessary for staff members to make portable reproductions of the specimens. A few intended for public exhibition were painted over plastered panels as described above. Most reproductions were half-size copies on heavy illustration board that could be kept in convenient portfolios. In the reproductions, zones that originally were naked wall areas surrounding designs were covered with masking tape while the rest were sprayed with a paint mixture made from dry pigments to match the Awatovi wall color. The masking tape removed, the panels were sprayed a second time to make the plaster area to be decorated appear darker. When that coating was dry, Davis, using a casein paint, followed field notes to trace in patterns.

With that step accomplished, Smith went off to war in the Pacific Theater of Operations and further work was halted.

Four years later it was back to the drawing boards. As Smith once again sat before tables strewn with the Awatovi mural reproductions, he must have felt dismay at the task of trying to bring order out of seeming chaos and frustration at not having larger samples with complete images with which to work. He sorted the illustration boards into piles of examples having shared characteristics. Only the Spanish-dictated ones were duplicates. After due consideration, he shuffled them again. And again. From their first sighting at Awatovi, Smith realized he was dealing with two categories of religious expressions. One was a window into the very soul of the Pueblo people. The other was mere decoration according to European taste and had no hidden significance. It was the prehistoric specimens that presented the greatest challenge, for how could he, an individual from a totally different cultural milieu separated from the Amerindic past by centuries, ever comprehend their meanings? As a matter of fact, even the Hopi workmen at the site could not recognize many of the images or explain their significance. It was not just the passage of time for them, but that sacred knowledge had been restricted to a select group of leaders and initiates. Only with total immersion and dogged determination for the next few years did Smith finally produce what amounts to milestones in the archaeological studies of the northern Southwest.

In 1949 the Peabody Museum published an important monograph on the mission of San Bernardo de Aguatubi, from which the name of the site is derived.[18] J. O. Brew described the excavations and reviewed the history of the Spaniards at Awatovi and elsewhere on the Colorado Plateau and in the Rio Grande valley. He took the account of the Spaniards from their first appearance in 1540 to the transfer of political power over

New Mexico to the newly established Mexican Republic in 1819, more than a century after Awatovi was sacked. Architect Ross Montgomery contributed the major work on the history of the Franciscan Order in New Spain and his ideas on the conjectural reconstruction of their large installation at Awatovi. Watson Smith concerned himself with the church wall paintings in comparison with the Hispanic tile tradition in motherland Spain and colonial Mexico. That was fairly easy going for Smith because the comparative sections primarily were searches of relevant literature. His contribution was significant, nevertheless, in bringing together background data that previously had been neglected due to the bias then held by regional archaeologists against consideration of historical materials.

Next came the hard part: the kiva murals. Smith was aware that he must review the natural and cultural background out of which they had evolved.

Surveys had shown that small hamlets and villages of agricultural peoples had been in the Jeddito since about 600, or Basketmaker III times. These farmers took advantage of springs along the southern base of the lofty Black Mesa landform to the north where sandstone capping dipping southward was a good aquifer. The region below that mesa looked like a desolate wasteland because of a thick mantle of fixed and free sand dunes. Today's Hopi say their ancestors settled there because no one else wanted the land.[19] In truth, those dunes were, and still are, critical to farmers. They retain deep moisture and curtail runoff. Many washes spewing down from Black Mesa to the south provide seasonal waters that fan out across the valleys.[20] Over many centuries farmers had hybridized a species of corn with exceedingly long root structure that reached down to tap into buried moisture and with a dwarf above-ground stalk that could withstand buffeting wind. The farmers helped nature along by placing rows of brush beside plants to act as windbreaks. Archaeologists now find in old garden plots lines of small stones that once held these screens in place.[21] Success at farming brought increased population, and lifestyle was comparable to that of fellow agriculturalists across the central Colorado Plateau. However, Jeddito dwellers were fortunate in escaping at least some of the hardships caused by environmental deterioration that plagued other areas in the latter years of the thirteenth century. They were able to stay put and would become the core of a new human realignment that developed over a century during which throngs of dislocated groups from the Four Corners to the north, the Little Colorado River valley to the south, and the flanks of the Grand Canyon to the west moved in with them. One of the new towns that grew from this influx was Awatovi.

Brew's archaeological efforts showed that Awatovi, begun as something of a refugee camp, endured for an estimated five hundred years. First a small contingent of what most likely were indigenous families and others sharing their architectural and ceramic conventions moved to the southern tip of Antelope Mesa. The boulder-strewn escarpment dropped off in front of their rooms (Fig. 29).[22] They had a grand view of the Jeddito valley below, the badlands of the Painted Desert out beyond, and off in the distance to the west the majestic San Francisco Peaks towering over a volcanic field that had been active just several centuries previously. They brought water for domestic use from several springs at the eastern foot of the mesa.[23] They probably planted crops in several environments in order to ensure returns in at least one locality. Such places were dunes on the mesa and around its base, Jeddito River floodplains, and arroyo mouths. Wide, double masonry walls that differed from what would be determined to be later construction and black-on-white pottery typical of the region led Brew to conclude that the initial occupation of what he called the West Mound had taken place near the close of the thirteenth century, or classic Pueblo III times.[24] The white-ware pottery type, named Tusayan Black-on-White, was tree-ring dated to ca. 1250–1300, but other archaeological evidence suggests a beginning production in the twelfth century.[25] A new pottery style appeared before this section of the site was vacated. It was Jeddito Black-on-Orange, partly a companion to the black-on-white type. It appeared about 1275 but continued as a transitional type into the early Pueblo IV period of the fourteenth century.[26] Both the black-on-white and black-on-orange types bore only geometric designs.

Gradually the original settlers were joined by others. The town grew steadily upward, rooms on top of buried rooms, to reach a level that in modern times created a hillock some twenty-five feet in height. The upper walls were constructed of only one course of masonry. More striking than the construction techniques was the emergence of a new kind of pottery that was yellow. That was a color achieved through exploitation of certain clays and high temperatures resulting from the use of coal as fuel for firing pottery.

What a discovery it must have been when some Hopi persons learned that coal would burn! Did lightning set brush on fire near one of the seams of coal exposed along the feet of Antelope Mesa or the Hopi Buttes? Did a chunk of coal being used as a hearth stone ignite? After existing for half a millennium next to one of the country's largest coal deposits, the Pueblos of Black Mesa must have been astounded by learning of the value of coal as fuel. Quickly it was being strip mined from outcrops along the Antelope Mesa escarpment and used to heat homes and to turn greenware into hard ceramics.[27]

The yellow pottery may not have originated specifically at Awatovi or the contemporary neighboring settlements, but it is identified with the Jeddito district. Shortly potters began to paint its plain ground with black pigment. Tree-ring dates center on 1300 but production continued for a century thereafter.[28]

As Awatovi continued to grow, the West Mound fell into ruin and new construction spread up the mesa to the north and east. Archaeological crews did limited testing in the central part of this expanded village, intending to devote more time to it in the future. That proved impossible due to cancellation of the excavation permit. They concentrated instead on the dwellings near the mission. They determined that in both these occupations potters had created an exciting new type that used black and red pigments over the yellow paste and that much of the design vocabulary echoed katsina iconography. Called Sikyatki Polychrome after a site at the base of First Mesa explored in the late nineteenth century, it was the rage for all Hopi potters through the fifteenth century.[29] By the time the Spaniards arrived, it was a vogue on the wane locally but continued as a viable trade item that was distributed far and wide.

Recognizing the yeasty cross-fertilization that Brew's work indicated, Smith's efforts to interpret the kiva wall paintings culminated in 1952. Peabody published his exhaustive, if wordy (he was a lawyer, after all), study entitled *Kiva Mural Decoration at Awatovi and Kawaika-a*.[30] The subtitle *With a Survey of Other Wall Paintings in the Pueblo Southwest* revealed a second contribution of importance. The author was satisfied that he could distinguish four groupings of drawings based upon composition and content. They were not mutually exclusive but varied in structure, scale, complexity, color, and symbolism.

Smith then examined those ceramics from the deposition in each of the excavated kivas to see if they suggested chronological order and, if so, did that jibe with his categories. Happily, they did.[31] The mural grouping exhibiting the least complex designs and format came from the upper-level West Mound kivas, including Room 218 where wall paintings were first discovered, an area Brew regarded as fourteenth century in date. It was a temporal phase called early Pueblo IV. The mural group having the most intricate layout was mainly that remaining in the kiva beneath the mission church, known from tree-ring dates read in roof timbers to belong to the sixteenth century, perhaps later. The most recent of these dates was 1504.[32] The recovered pottery primarily was of late Pueblo IV local types. Possibly a three-hundred-year wall painting tradition was represented. The final stage was one showing great virtuosity, but even in the earliest examples of this art there was no evident beginners' ineptitude.

It was this quality of consummate skill on the part of the artists, whether the wall paintings were early or late in the sequence, that greatly impressed Smith. Always sure handed and deft, these artists painted lines that were straight where desired, curved with grace, jagged if necessary. But always they were the same width throughout, never carelessly thick and thin, never wavering. Filler colors, often used without regard to reality, never spilled over outlines. Smith found no hint of the use of patterns or cartoons for the various panels, no preliminary sketching in of layouts, no indication of corrections. In contrast, overseas fifteenth-century Europeans customarily designed their works on sheets of paper pasted together, pricked them, and then pounced the motifs onto the walls or copied them directly on the plaster using charcoal or red ochre. It was mind-boggling to think of one or several individuals standing before a long blank wall and, drawing only upon deep reserves of mental focus and uninhibited free-wheeling imagination, taking up brushes to create emblematic scenes depicting messengers to the gods, their perceived accouterments, and their burden of prayers. José Clemente Orozco, eminent Mexican muralist of the period in which Smith worked, would have been astounded. He wrote, "The artist, forced by strict discipline, must find out beforehand exactly what he wants to do and must prepare his designs and materials with thoroughness before the actual execution."[33] But there was a valid explanation for Pueblo success.

For several millennia Pueblo craftsmen and craftswomen demonstrated considerable talents in technical and aesthetic works. Yet, during the eras leading up to these late-thirteenth-century demographic shifts, even though their graphic arts remained of high quality, they had become generally uninspired. For example, potters continued the basic geometrical grammar that had been ubiquitous for centuries. Just occasionally did they slip in a naturalistic element. Only in areas south of the San Juan River did they produce red paste polychrome wares in addition to the traditional black-on-whites. These, too, bore only geometric patterning. The wall paintings at Lowry Ruin typify that craft at the Pueblo III stage, or ca. 1100–1300. The panels of terraced white-on-brown elements were pleasing but certainly not novel or exciting to adults who had seen them since infancy on various media. It seemed that the responsible artisans were coasting along content with the status quo. The people had held animistic beliefs since antiquity, and they expressed these beliefs through etchings and monochromatic and polychromatic paintings upon rocky surfaces in all corners of the plateau. Such works, thought to have been supplications to a host of supernaturals, included human and animal figures portrayed both relatively realistically and fantastically. Undoubtedly the Pueblos had a deep-seated love of drama and costuming about which we know little. All these facets of religious undercurrents continued to be celebrated in the kivas, but whatever they were ultimately did not appear adequate to forestall hard times.

Then came the stimulation of a new religious surge that induced dramatic changes in outlook and offered loaded opportunities for artistic and theatrical demonstrations. Together with more secure environmental conditions, this impulse may have been the greatest magnet of all that ultimately attracted already troubled folks into the Hopi sphere.

Smith's four mural categories reflect an evolutionary process that was followed by successive generations of painters. As at Kuaua, they resorted to their known natural world to convey their unknown spiritual world. Earlier related peoples to the south in the Mimbres area of New Mexico had given vent to their beliefs in pottery design. Something of that outlook may have infused the new Hopi art. The human form, the goods of daily life, animals and plants, and environmental forces composed the foundation from which Awatovians worked. Sometimes they drew realistic images. Sometimes the patterns were combinations of real and mythical, the latter emphasized by mismatched body parts, adjoined fauna of several species, or fauna with humans, and nonsensical color combinations. Sometimes they were totally imaginary and baffling. Other times they were simply abstract themes from nature. Because of the gloom within kivas, with a single smoke-hole opening for daylight or firelight from a hearth at night, all must have taken on an unsettling eeriness that seems appropriate when dealing with the deities. That intangible essence of mystery disappeared upon removal of the paintings from their intended environment.

In the earliest attempts at wall painting at Awatovi, one simple large-scale motif made up an unframed panel. Not too dissimilar from pictograph and petroglyph renderings, generally it was a zoomorph;[34] that is, an animal form not depicted realistically and probably considered a

Fig. 39. *Late-thirteenth- to early-fourteenth-century zoomorph representing earliest style of Awatovi mural painting. The figure is white and has black teeth and two red eyes on the same side of the head. Because of the long tail over the body, Smith regarded it as a mountain lion. The white oval was a wall niche in which offerings likely were placed.*

god. One little creature of this style was drawn with both eyes on the same side of the head (Fig. 39). A few elements recall birds or small animals. Paintings of this initial period lack human or anthropomorphic figures or items used in rituals. This suggests that at the threshold of the fourteenth century the programs of the katsina cult had not yet been fully conceptualized and that artists were repeating traditional devices.

Gradually painters began to enclose their panels by drawing one large rectangle across the wall space and filling it in with a background color. The effect was rather like a blank framed canvas prepared for oil paint-

Fig. 40. Portion of a Sikyatki-style abstract pattern characterizing Smith's second-to-oldest mural category at Awatovi. An anthropomorph with a clawed human leg, recurved tail, and tail feathers is lost in a complexity of abstractions. At far right is an upright tiponi, or feather-encased ear of corn.

ing. The space was crowded with intricate conventional designs that duplicated those appearing contemporaneously on the local Sikyatki Polychrome pottery.[35] Common motifs densely laid on were bird feathers and wings and sweeping scrolls arranged around a circular element, making it appear that an attempt was being made to imitate decoration at the mouths of pottery jars (Fig. 40). Humans or anthropomorphs with their paraphernalia still had not become part of the visual repertoire. The time frame likely was late 1300s.

Category three includes works from a period that saw major stylistic

Fig. 41. Human figure of undetermined sex in full black garment with typical white linear patterning. The legs are blue, and the arms and face are yellow. Smith assigned this depiction to his second-most-recent category.

developments, obviously as a result of accruing confidence and skill on the part of the artists and perhaps a firmer commitment to, and elaboration of, the cult practices. Anthropomorphic and human figures slightly less than life size make their colorful appearance. They are attended by an elaborate inventory of material items. In Smith's analysis they express animation, vigor, and boldness. Figures are dressed in what must have been special garments of the day (Fig. 41). Perhaps most interesting are eleven figures out of a total of twenty-one that could be recognized, despite their fragmentary condition, as warriors in combat.[36] They face each other in adversarial positions. Some are falling as if wounded. All are accompanied by shields, bows and arrows, or quivers. By then a War Society apparently was part of the cult organization to which the paint-

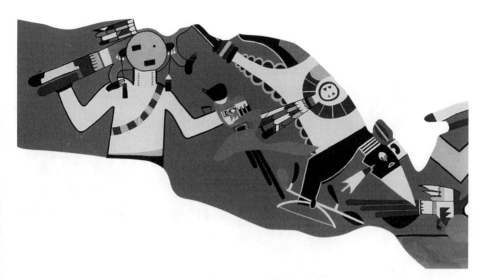

Fig. 42. Portion of one of the most recent animated Awatovi panels. Smith re-garded the figure on the right, head down and holding a sun shield and bear-ing a bear paw symbol on the cheek, as possibly a Hopi Twin War God. The masked figure on the left is not identified.

ings must refer (Fig. 42). On the other hand, some so-called shields may have been strictly symbolic ceremonial paraphernalia such as would have been used in enactments of ritualized struggles (Fig. 43). One won-ders if the mid to late 1400s was an especially disturbed time due to in-ternal conflicts or nomadic pressures. As yet archaeology does not con-firm this.

A peak in the series of Awatovi murals occurred during the sixteenth century when comparable panels with baseline and vertical dividers spread across all four walls of the kivas. The field of design had become structured. Smith suggests that such compartmentalization might indi-cate either framing on the wall behind an altar set up in front or a substi-tute for that feature. The drawing is controlled and balanced. Identi-fiable human or anthropomorphic figures number sixty, nine of which

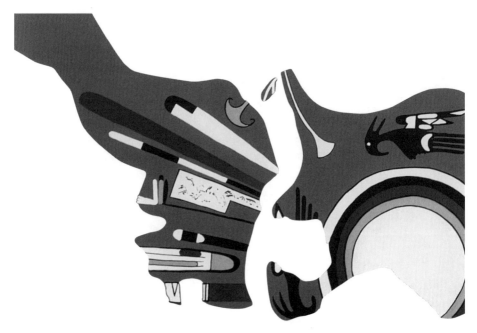

Fig. 43. *So-called Sun Shield assigned to category 3. The white center is en-circled by salmon, red, black, and white rings. Radiating feathers and prayer plumes and birds in profile complete the pattern.*

are large and legless, their torsos resting on the baseline.[37] Whether with legs or without, the figures are fancifully dressed. Some faces are defi-nitely masked, but others may be merely painted. Smith believed he could identify a few specific katsinas among them. However, he did not attempt the ideological interpretations later explored by Dutton in the Kuaua paintings. Smith regarded all figures of this phase as passive and unlike their active counterparts in the previous stage. A parade of natural and mythical small and large animals, birds, frogs, and insects is present. So too are many objects taken from everyday routines. These include netted gourds, pottery medicine bowls, sticks used in rabbit hunts, prayer sticks, pipes, medallions, and ears of corn. To Smith the impression im-parted by the late panels was one of placidity. Perhaps they mirror a time of tranquility when the gods were hearing the prayers for rain brought by the katsinas even though the usual rain symbols of clouds, rainbows, or lightning are rare.

Because the first of the Jeddito murals were uncovered a year after the findings at Kuaua, Smith had the opportunity to make comparative analyses. He regarded the work of artists in both regions as sharing the same religious outlook. However, the paintings at Kuaua came from a single kiva and likely were done by members of one society over a relatively short period of time. Those at Awatovi and Kawaika-a were in twenty-five kivas, in the case of the former erected and used during the course of perhaps as much as three centuries. Kuaua murals, though fewer in number, were less eroded. These distinctions weaken comparisons. Nevertheless, there is an obvious static quality to the Kuaua paintings. Frontal figures are lined up in a row, seemingly oblivious to each other. They resemble Pueblo line dancers in arrangement, dress, and lack of expression and animation. There is no formalization of the design field other than two examples of a ground line. Common elements not generally used at Awatovi are growing corn, rain symbols, masked faces, and horned serpents. Some observers believe these differences signify a vague Mexican influence that was more pronounced in the central Rio Grande district than in Hopiland.[38] The Sikyatki modes, elaborate embroidered and tie-dyed garments, movement of figures, and structured layout were more typical of Awatovian renditions.[39] Although broadly contemporaneous in the 1400s and 1500s, some complex work at Awatovi apparently was more recent than that at Kuaua and extended into the Spanish period. And it could be that artists there simply were more skilled and advanced in their craft.

The murals confirm that competency in textile arts was another contribution to the evolving Hopi lifeway that fourteenth-century immigrants from all surrounding regions brought in their cultural baggage. The vertical loom was one item in an associated complex of introductions. That device and the cotton that could be woven with it made important impacts on the local social and economic systems that continued well into the historic period.

Some botanists believe that cotton diffused through the Western Hemisphere from northern coastal Peru, to where it somehow had spread from its native Asia. It evolved as it spread, adapting to the growing seasons and elevations of various environments. One species came via western Mexico into the Southwest early in the Christian Era.[40] By 700 Hohokam peoples in the Arizona deserts were trading dry bolls of cotton northward to the Colorado Plateau. This commodity was advantageous to the traders because it was lightweight for easy transport and it represented fiber and seed food to potential users.

According to archaeological findings, some four or so centuries later cotton was being raised in favorable areas of the northern Southwest and traded from there to other parts of the territory. The species *Gossypium hopii* was a plant that could be cultivated outside the usual range for cotton because it required a growing season as brief as eighty-four to one hundred frost-free days.[41]

Research within the past decade at a series of sites near Winslow on the Little Colorado River has produced such a volume of cotton pollen and seeds in flotation samples that archaeologists working there think it was a mainstay of the occupation. They theorize that raw cotton was exported to the Hopi settlements to the north, such as Awatovi, in exchange for Jeddito ceramics.[42] If so, this is a unique example of prehistoric entrepreneurship based upon production of a plant whose primary use may not have been as a foodstuff.

These Little Colorado River sites, now incorporated into Homolovi State Park, were abandoned about 1400 or somewhat earlier. Some of the residents likely moved to the Jeddito and Hopi mesas. It is not known if cotton was actually being raised there before their arrival, but it is of interest that clothing shows up on mural figures of just this time. It seems certain that by the 1400s cotton was planted together with the triumvirate of corn, beans, and squash along the floodplains by the Jeddito River and at the mouths of the many arroyos feeding into it where runoff waters could wet garden plots. Hough reported cotton seeds in deposits at Kawaika-a.[43] Physiographer John Hack, on the Awatovi expedition staff, felt that for these farmers cotton was second only to corn.[44] Crotty suggests that a design motif of circular elements stacked in bowls may have represented cotton rather than corn.[45]

Proof that the vertical loom was added to the list of commonly used objects exists in the form of spaced anchor holes that the diggers found in kiva floors.[46] Brew also considered some shaped stones with recesses for gripping to have been loom weights.[47] A long wooden top bar for a loom would have been fastened to the kiva roof timbers, and the bottom bar would have been held in place by cordage through loops secured in those floor holes. Weavers would have pulled warp fibers taut from top to bottom. It is hard to understand why they put looms in such darkened rooms, where seeing fine work must have been difficult. Perhaps these surroundings were cleaner than dwelling rooms filled with children, dogs, and cooking fumes and where space was at a minimum. Regardless, weaving became a male activity in the kivas.

According to Kate Peck Kent, a leading authority on prehistoric Southwestern textiles, it was the job of the men who were doing the weaving to prepare the cotton for use.[48] They ginned the bolls by picking out the seeds. Then to card the smashed wads on a pile of clean sand, they used a fanlike whip of four or five sticks bound together at one end for beating the wads until they were fluffy and scoured by the sand. Next they spun the fibers into thread by twisting them together, using a spindle whorl on a rod. This simple process produced one-ply thread, which generally was left white. Sometimes weavers used either a vegetal or mineral solution to dye the thread. Brown, red, and black were the most common colors. Yellow and bluish gray threads were less popular.

Kiva sizes were such that usually no more than several looms could be strung up at a time. One can visualize men seated on the floor of the kiva in front of their looms, working with their wefts and battens, enjoying companionship while they talked over the affairs of the day. Over the course of the fifteenth century they and those who followed them became the most accomplished weavers of all the Pueblo tribes. When the Spaniards arrived, they were impressed with the Jeddito fields of cot-

Fig. 44. Probable cotton blanket pattern. Colors are mottled gray and white.

ton and the volume and quality of textiles that were the end products
(Fig. 44). Cotton blankets were especially prized.

These textiles were illustrated in the Awatovi murals as clothing on
the human and anthropomorphic figures and are particularly important
because so few examples of prehistoric clothes have been recovered.[49]
The garments were not the breechcloths farmers wore when they went
to hoe their gardens. Nor were they the fringed aprons housewives had
on when they took their water jars to the spring. What they were was ceremonial garb made from the finest fabrics the weavers could create as
something fit for the katsinas. Kent considered cloth shirts, garters, hair
ties, possible socks, and blanket dresses — one piece of cloth from the
knees to the underarms — as of Pueblo origin. Twill, tapestry, and plain
weaves were part of that tradition. So, too, were the tie-dying and painting of plain cloth techniques that allowed unrestricted patterning. Kent
credited the inspiration for openwork shirts, braided sashes, and kilts
with elaborate tassels and embroidered borders to Hohokam sources

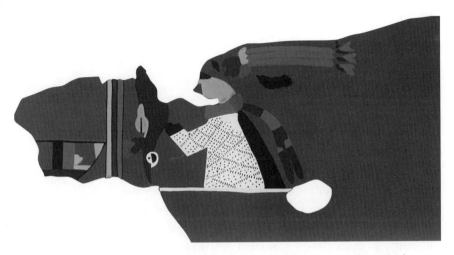

Fig. 45. Awatovi figure in profile wears upper white garment that may have been of a netting technique derived from Hohokam sources. The headdress streaming out behind was red, yellow, blue, and green feathers. A green scarf with green and red end designs encircles the neck.

(Fig. 45).[50] The kilt, which became a ubiquitous garment in the north, often was enriched with an embroidered lower edge of designs shared with Jeddito pottery.

The practice of the katsina cult led to what was a men's club. If anthropological wisdom is correct, women were barred from kivas at times of secret ceremonies. Therefore, it stands to reason that the muralists were masculine. They were producing sacred images in restricted quarters. Perhaps there was craft specialization at work, with a few particularly gifted initiates chosen, on behalf of the kiva's society, to be messengers through their art to the katsina messengers to the gods. Women were permitted to witness the rituals held in the enclosed plazas in which all the masked dancers were male. There were female katsinas, but in ceremonies men impersonated them. As to the murals with their assemblage of figures, only three at Awatovi can be considered as feminine. One, naked and prone on her back, is about to be penetrated by an aroused male. This is the sole bit of pornography in the collection. Another figure has the body of a squash and arms of leafed stems but what might be a female head. A somewhat similar rendition appears in the Kuaua collection. In the kiva beneath the church one head, body weathered away, is that of an unmarried maiden with the traditional whorl of hair over each ear.[51]

In spite of what at least superficially can be interpreted as some sort of policy that prevented women from active roles in the katsina cult, they obviously knew something of its metaphysical side. This is evidenced by their Sikyatki Polychrome ceramic designs, which included katsina cult icons. Those likely were applied freehand without the benefit of patterns and with the same controlled expertise shown by the male muralists.

Archaeologist Charles Adams, for a number of years working with Hopi and middle Little Colorado River materials, theorizes that the katsina cult, as it came to be formulated, first arose among peoples living in the upper reaches of the Little Colorado River.[52] This is a wide zone that in his definition stretches across central Arizona and New Mexico from about Holbrook to east of Acoma Pueblo. Plazas bordered on at least two sides by dwellings and rectangular kivas, both features considered necessary adjuncts for defining the cult, were present there. These traits and the design format for Four Mile Polychrome pottery likely had originated among tribes as far south as northern Mexico. From that upper Little Colorado River hearth, Adams sees the cult being introduced to the Hopi about 1325.[53] That would coincide with the end of Smith's earliest wall painting category.

The katsina cult was readily accepted by the Hopi because, in Adams's view, it was the adhesive that held a large heterogeneous population together in relative harmony. One reason for its strength was that all could participate at some level regardless of clan membership, which tended to pit one group against another. A second reason was that the cult's dominant theme was prayer for the rains that meant life itself in this harsh land. The Hopi, beneficiaries of the artistic abilities of so many diverse peoples, soon elaborated the cult's observable components to encompass wall paintings such as those at Awatovi and Kawaika-a.

In 1975, the fortieth anniversary of the initiation of the Awatovi project, some of the Anglo and Hopi survivors made a nostalgic return to

Fig. 46. Fortieth reunion, in 1975, of Hopi men and scientists who had parti-
cipated in the Awatovi expeditions: (a) Front row, left to right: Pat Williams,
Emory Coochwikvia, Kenneth Polacca, Gibson Namoki, Max Namoki, Eric
Lalo, Sylvan Nash; back row, left to right: Al Lancaster, Dick Wheeler,
Watson Smith.

the site. They celebrated the old days and renewed friendships that had
linked them through the years (Fig. 46a–c).

It is proper that today the works of aboriginal Hopi imagery—which
developed over centuries in northern Arizona and made Awatovi famous
in archaeological history—have come home. The bulk of the Awatovi
mural collection, original and reproduced, has been returned by the
Peabody Museum and now is curated in the Museum of Northern Arizona in Flagstaff. The colored copies made by Penny Davis and contained in fourteen large portfolios remain as brilliant as when she ex-
pertly executed them nearly a half century ago. Four original panels,
very dim and less discernible, are intact. They were shown for a time on
the walls of a Museum of Northern Arizona replica of a semisubterranean, rectangular kiva. Unfortunately, the modern kiva roof leaked, no
doubt unintentionally copying the fifteenth-century state of affairs. The

Fig. 46. (b) Watson Smith in fore-ground; behind, Stanley Olsen, Emory Coochwikvia, Al Lancaster.

Fig. 46. (c) Al Lancaster and Kenneth Polacca.

vulnerable murals were removed to storage with one exception, which is mounted under glass in the museum hall. Visitors walk by, perhaps glance at it, and, beyond doubt, have little appreciation for the depth of emotion and belief it represents nor even the artistic abilities or powers of imagination displayed by peoples of an earlier time. Nor could the visitors possibly know of the labors and pleasures of those who helped save it from total extinction. If a Hopi artist familiar with the ancient mural painting technique can be persuaded to again periodically paint the now blank kiva walls, then interest in it and this intriguing part of the Hopi past may be rekindled for both Native Americans and those of us who benefit from knowledge of this priceless heritage.

To further this understanding, the staff members of the Peabody Museum, the Museum of Northern Arizona, and the Hopi tribe, together with a few outside scholars, hope to record images on some six hundred known extant Sikyatki Polychrome vessels scattered through many diverse collections and compare them with those images appearing in the Awatovi-Kawaika-a wall paintings. Such a study might reveal the degree of linkage between these two aesthetic expressions executed by contemporary female and male artisans working under the same religious inspiration.[54]

Today the ruins of Awatovi sleep away on the Hopi Reservation. Formerly visitors could go to the site with a tribal guide. At this writing, the site is closed to the public.

Notes

1. Brew, 1937.
2. Descriptions of camp life are to be found in Smith, 1992, and Smith n.d.
3. Brew, 1937, 125, 134; Hough, 1903, Pl. 89.
4. Smith, 1952, Fig. 34c; Smith, 1972, Fig. 70.
5. Brew, 1937, 135.
6. Smith, 1952, Fig. 46a.
7. Smith, 1980, 30.
8. Brew, 1949a, Pt. I, Fig. 22d; Smith, 1972, 63–64, Figs. 40–41.
9. Smith, 1952, 317.
10. Brew, 1939, 126, 134.
11. Smith, 1952; Smith 1980, 31–32.
12. Smith, 1980, 31.
13. Ibid., 33.
14. Ibid., 33–34.
15. Smith, 1949, 303–305, Fig. 55.
16. Ibid., Figs. 59, 61a–c.
17. Brew, 1937, 137; Brew 1952, ix.
18. Montgomery, Smith, and Brew, 1949.
19. Trimble, 1993, 48.
20. Hack, 1942a, 12–15.
21. Ibid., Pl. Vf, VIa.
22. Brew, 1937, Pls. 4–5.
23. Hack, 1942a, 14, Fig. 8.
24. Brew, 1937, 129–130.

25. Breternitz, 1966, 99.

26. Ibid., 78; Brew, 1937, 131.

27. Brew, 1937, 130; Hack, 1942a; 1942b.

28. Breternitz, 1966, 78.

29. Ibid., 95.

30. Smith, 1952.

31. Ibid., 315–317.

32. Ibid., 317.

33. Hale, 1966, Preface.

34. Smith, 1952, Fig. 43.

35. Ibid., Figs. 48–49, Pl. H.

36. Ibid., Figs. 52–54.

37. Ibid., Figs. 80b, 81a-b, 84b, Pls. F, I.

38. Schaafsma and Schaafsma, 1974, 535–545.

39. Smith, 1952, 150–151.

40. Kent, 1957, 467.

41. Hack, 1942a, 36, Fig. 4.

42. E. C. Adams, 1991, 175, 181–183.

43. Hough, 1903, 345.

44. Hack, 1942a, 19–20.

45. Crotty, 1995, 192–193.

46. Smith, 1972, 121–122.

47. Brew, 1937, 125.

48. Kent, 1957, 470–474.

49. Ibid., Fig. 142; Smith, 1952, 171, Fig. 24.

50. Kent, 1957, 647, Table 11.

51. Smith,. 1952, Figs. 53b, 61b, 78a, Pl. A.

52. E. C. Adams, 1991, 120, 185, 190.

53. Ibid., 190.

54. L. J. Kuwanwisiwma, director, Cultural Preservation Office, the Hopi Tribe, memorandum to the Crow Canyon Archaeological Center, July 29, 1999 (Archives, Crow Canyon Archaeological Center, Cortez, Colorado).

Metaphors on the Puerco

The plain-talking ranchers on the Rio Puerco of central New Mexico called a local physiographic anomaly Pottery Mound because that was what it was: elevated hummocks of earth, sand, and stunted grass thickly paved with millions of ceramic fragments. Unimaginative though the name was, it guaranteed archaeological interest. Other than the prominent rise above a broad, barren floodplain that probably is exaggerated because of modern entrenchment of the river's course, the mounds themselves were unimpressive (Figs. 47, 48). Before recent disturbance, any visual evidence of old constructions was lacking. However, the abundance of pottery that crushed under foot like corn flakes was a clue to considerable former human presence there and could be counted upon to provide temporal and cultural information.

When old homes and sanctuaries of the ancient Pueblos of the Rio Grande were abandoned, they melted into oblivion, burying whatever castoffs those who moved on had left behind. Experience said there were heavy stone implements, bone tools, worn sandals, cumbersome pots of clay, and other residues of living and dying under what became a pre-

Fig. 47. *Looking northeast across the Pottery Mound site on the west terrace above the entrenched Rio Puerco; temporary excavation ramada in foreground.*

historic landfill cleansed by drifts of hard clods and windblown earth and embroidered by accents of prickly tumbleweeds. There is the sadness of dashed hopes and despair resonating through such places, but forlorn scenes of silent desertion are an inescapable part of Southwestern landscapes. Human life there, whether of the undocumented vales of antiquity or of yesterday, always has been insecure.

It may seem strange that fractured earthenware containers in particular could have much importance in the interpretation of nuances of human history. But for scientists working with pottery-producing peoples in the prehistoric Southwest, humble vessels fashioned from the earth itself are invaluable research tools. One primary reason for pottery's importance is its durability. Given the low-fired and hence friable nature of the pottery, and given the mode of past living on the ground without the benefit of furniture or cupboards in which to store fragile objects,

Fig. 48. View to south across the Rio Puerco; remains of Pottery Mound with Ladron Mountains in background.

whole vessels were easily broken. Their shattered remains, however, are forever because they are resistant to fire, water, sand blasting, bacteria, and other destructive forces. They survive when more perishable, perhaps more significant, artifacts disappear. Moreover, the ancestral Pueblo women, once they realized how pottery facilitated their domestic routines, became extremely proficient and prolific in the craft. Added to the scientific advantage of having great quantities of such materials to study is the ability to coordinate those materials with tree-ring dating. Precise calendric positioning had become a reality that was unbelievable just a few short years before Pottery Mound was recognized as an archaeological zone. Furthermore, by that time sufficient ceramic study had been done so that stylistic variations through time could be pinpointed. This made it possible to trace otherwise obscure interactions between various of the groups who once lived upon this land.

Knowing of Pottery Mound and recognizing its importance to an understanding of the prehistory of the central Rio Grande area, Frank Hibben, faculty member of the University of New Mexico, in the early

1950s decided it would be an appropriate place to conduct a summer archaeological field school. The surface pottery suggested a Pueblo IV settlement. In the more easterly Rio Grande corridor slicing through the heartland of New Mexico, two and a half centuries of European occupation had obliterated or gutted sites of that period. Few whites other than a handful of cattlemen had moved westward across the bleak Puerco valley or its uplands, looting antiquities as they went. That made Pottery Mound a prime research target. Further, Smith's definitive report on the Awatovi and Kawaika-a murals recently had been published. Hibben must have hoped that if the Hopi had engaged in wall painting, so too had their coeval neighbors to the east.

The years of World War II, with Allied troops spread around the world and into contact with cultures and places about which they had little former knowledge, brought about a lively watershed period in Southwestern archaeology. Whereas before the war only a few institutions offered degrees in anthropology, shortly thereafter there were ten or more. Many of these saw student field schools as a necessary part of the curriculum, providing practical hands-on experience in exploratory procedures while at the same time generating fees and labor to accomplish specific research goals. In practical terms, field schools are not the ideal way to accomplish research. Although instruction is their primary aim, the field schools generally run for just a month or six weeks, while a project can extend over a number of sessions before the desired investigatory results are achieved. Nevertheless, the administrators of the University of New Mexico—which under Hewett and his successors had played a leading pioneer role in offering archaeological field schools—thought the time was ripe to resume the activity. Hence, for six seasons between 1954 and 1962 Hibben nominally directed that program at Pottery Mound.

Because Pottery Mound is located just thirty-five miles southwest of Albuquerque, it was not necessary to set up a field camp. Participants lived on campus or nearby and daily were transported to the dig by bus or came in their personal vehicles. That eliminated any daydreams the students may have had about mounting an expedition and marching off into the wilderness. The last few miles of the route to the dig were

Fig. 49. *Uncertain transportation to Pottery Mound.*

parallel tire tracks on ranch lands that wound over gravel terraces, down sandy arroyos, and across the Puerco. Not infrequently the bus had difficulty in negotiating this alleged road. Pushing it out of deep ruts was the closest thing to adventure these mostly citified young people experienced (Fig. 49).

No additional labor crew was hired to work at Pottery Mound. The

Fig. 50. Dig boss Gwinn Vivian instructing University of New Mexico field school students at Pottery Mound, 1957.

students did the digging. Some were hefty football players, giving rise to a joke about being accepted because they could move lots of dirt and not because of any special interest in the Indian past. For all, it was groveling in the hard earth, tediously troweling, baking under a relentless summer sun, and nursing blisters. The girls in their shorts reveled in their suntans, little aware in those days before sunscreen that they were flirt-

Fig. 51. Student cook-out; Gwinn Vivian tending barbeque, Frank Hibben observing at left.

ing with one of those health hazards afforded by the harsh Southwestern environment.

Even with these drawbacks, the students, as young people are wont to do, imparted to the sessions a feeling of summer-camp fun with ongoing horseplay, raucous banter, romances, and carefree weekend trips to archaeological sites. Gwinn Vivian, Gordon's son and one of a series of graduate-student dig bosses, recalls instructing the novices in excavation methods, cooking over camp fires on outings, and trying to keep some order among the students and their field notes (Figs. 50, 51). One episode that stands out in his memory involved having to call a male student down from a dangerously high photographic platform (Fig. 52). It seems said student had climbed up the scaffold with the expedition's expensive surveying alidade to spy on several females who were skinny dipping in a stock tank during their lunch break. Archaeology gone pleasantly off course. With college students, of course.

The site of Pottery Mound Pueblo reaches along the west bank of the

Fig. 52. *Looking up through photographic scaffolding used at Pottery Mound excavations.*

Rio Puerco drainage. The Spanish word *río* and its English equivalent *river* are used loosely in the Southwest. In most places they connote running water, but not so here. Commonly they merely mean a drainage that may be bone dry most of the time, carry a slow moving trickle after spring thaws, or channel a raging torrent for an hour or two after summer cloudbursts. The Rio Puerco is of this type and, because it drains decidedly down to the Rio Grande depression, often overflows. At the time of occupation, the community of Pottery Mound Pueblo probably was just back from the intermittent stream. Entrenchment since that time has left it on a bluff above that continues to crumble downslope (Figs. 47,

48). Puerco translates to "dirty," a clue to its relentless downcutting. The treeless high desert surrounding the locality stretches east toward the trough of the Rio Grande and beyond to the Manzano Mountains. To the south the Ladron Mountains scratch the sky near Socorro. Rising along the western horizon toward the Continental Divide are broken, wooded mesas and encapsulated valleys that are the homeland of the Acoma tribe.

The Puerco district has supported humans for at least four or more millennia. Archaic hunters and gatherers camped on its dunes and gravel terraces. Out of this background slowly emerged the cultural expression of the ancestral Pueblos. At the end of the first millennium before Christ, hamlets of sedentary farmers were scattered here and there along the watercourse.

Subsequently, in a pattern common in southern portions of the Colorado Plateau, many of these hamlets and villages were deserted as, for unknown reasons, the people began to come together in large communities. This phenomenon of extensive population coalescence is one scholars now call aggregation. The Pottery Mound Pueblo was such a center. Its ultimate size and population remain to be determined but, as far as is known now, it was the largest community in the vicinity. The student diggers totally or partially cleared about 175 adobe-walled, contiguous rooms of it, leaving much of the site scientifically unexplored.[1] In places the houseblocks may have been several stories in height. The excavation of these units demanded considerable physical exertion, which allowed the football players to shine! Spot excavation in scattered portions of the site does not afford a clear picture of the overall ground plan. Apparently the knot of dwellings had grown upward and outward through time, with earlier cells filled and later ones placed over them without regard to former wall orientation. There seem to have been three or four enclosed plazas where ceremonies could have taken place. Although the core community was on the upper crust of the mound or dug into it, other units had been placed on its slopes or on lower ground around it.

Before the field school activity at Pottery Mound was terminated, Hibben had a backhoe cut a deep trench diagonally through the south part of the mound.[2] The careful use of such mechanical equipment had become accepted practice by this time in order to save enormous amounts of time and effort. The profile of the trench revealed an expansive clay and trash stratum beneath, and differing from, the ground surface. Some observers felt it was a lens naturally laid down in the distant past by the meandering river. Doubters argued that the depth of deposition and its configuration did not support such a premise. Another suggestion was that it was a man-made terrace on which to locate dwellings above flood level. That such waters were a threat was evident during the 1950s in the washing away of two small ruins near the edge of the arroyo. Potential danger would have been even greater if the large community and the river formerly were at the same level. However, the degree of downcutting was not determined. To Hibben this deposit was a two-tiered, flat-topped pyramid erected by Mexican migrants who intended to place a ceremonial center on it. Without further ado, he assured himself of a Mesoamerican-style structure measuring 215 feet on a side with a set of steps leading to its top. He had no explanation for the absence of any apparent building on its crest. Few colleagues were ready to accept this interpretation without more extensive explorations and geomorphological studies. Hibben also thought there was an associated Mexican ballcourt, but no definitive excavations of that part of the site were undertaken.[3] The unequivocal use of the words *pyramid* (rather than platform or terrace, for example) and *ballcourt* was reckless language apt to convey exotic features for which there was no proof.

Students learned that the pottery they took from their trenches and house cubicles duplicated that on the mound surface. Predominately it was of a single type manufactured in the late 1300s and first half of the 1400s.[4] It was a deep red ware decorated with geometric bands drawn with a lead pigment that vitrified and turned black upon being fired. Archaeologists know it as Glaze I or Glaze A, the first style in a long production of such pottery. Most scholars now think that the glaze-decorated earthenware tradition originated in the upper Little Colorado

River or Zuni-Cibola areas and diffused eastward, where it was copied by potters in the upper and central Rio Grande pueblos such as that at Pottery Mound. Trade ceramics recovered were the Jeddito yellow and Sikyatki polychromes made by Hopi artists of the same period. The four tree-ring dates detected in wood samples likewise established this site as an example of the early Pueblo IV horizon. Hibben proposed a 175-year occupation, which probably is too long.[5] Regardless, even a century-long presence means that four or five generations found life on the Puerco to be satisfying, with time enough to enjoy a rich ritualism.

For it was not the pottery for which the site was named that made Pottery Mound special. Instead, it was colorful paintings on the walls of fifteen rectangular kivas of Western Pueblo style and one large circular kiva of Eastern Pueblo style. One kiva had been sunk into refuse. Its walls were of wattle-and-daub (pole and mud) construction that collapsed when the deposition within the room was removed, taking some murals with them. One plaster layer was decorated with an interesting panel of alternating seated males shown in right-side views and seated quadrupeds identified as mountain lions also depicted in profile. Several of the mural fragments were saved, one of which Hibben gave to his friend William Fulton of the Amerind Foundation in Dragoon, Arizona.[6] Two of the structural pine poles were tree-ring dated to the early 1400s.[7]

Many kivas contained a wall niche for offerings such as that observed at Kuaua and in some Jeddito chambers. A local idiosyncrasy was the occasional low tunnel between the kiva and an adjacent room. These tunnels were not of a height comparable to those of some Pueblo III examples.

Because field school sessions were brief and the expense of removal and preservation of murals was considerable, Hibben elected to process the majority of the paintings in situ. Only a few fragments were saved for exhibition purposes. No new methods or materials for treating such fragile works had been devised since the 1930s work at Awatovi, nor did the project attempt any experimentation. Precise information is not available about procedures used at Pottery Mound, but presumably again it

Fig. 53. Sikyatki-style panel at Pottery Mound executed in black, white, and brown, showing relationship between the coeval Pottery Mound and Hopi villages.

was a matter of slowly scraping off successive adobe plaster coats until the base wall was reached. Photographs show that female students were assigned this task of delicately exposing the paintings.[8] They likely were particularly careful with their palette knives and are said to have been horrified to observe Brownie Hibben, Frank's wife, attack some scaling panels with a butcher knife she brought from home. Student artists photographed and copied the revealed designs as work continued, the importance of their work underscored by the successive eradication of original layers.

From the outset it was obvious that in most regards these wall paintings complemented those discovered twenty years earlier at Awatovi and were an integral part of katsina rites. Because the paintings were applied over base walls of adobe rather than rough-surfaced stone masonry, no preliminary wall preparation other than rubbing them smooth had been necessary. The fine-grained, well-puddled plaster, the decorative

Fig. 54. Squash body representing female form with maiden hairdo and partially masked face. Colors used are black, white, rust, tan, and yellow. The squash motif also was used at Awatovi.

pigments, the manner of execution, and some specific portrayals were familiar. Generally the imagery related to Smith's second and third stylistic categories. Some panels were of the Sikyatki Polychrome abstract vogue, or late 1300s in date (Fig. 53). Others included animated human, anthropomorphic, and zoomorphic figures of the 1400s (Figs. 54, 55).

Expectedly there were variations in content. Some differences were due to the geographical location of Pottery Mound, situated as a crossroads between a route of amorphous diffusion from Mexico up the Rio Grande and an actual northward movement of people out of the basin and range Mogollon territory. Earlier some Mogollon potters in the Mimbres area had demonstrated remarkable abilities at metaphorical figural art, and their descendants must have brought that as a gift to

*Fig. 55. Idiosyncratic treatment of presumably fe-
male figure at Pottery Mound. This local treatment
involved covering the upper torso and face with
densely placed black or red dots, as in this example.
The figure's only garb consists of a black device sug-
gesting breast encasements. In other renditions, the
upper body is bare but is painted with clustered dots,
which Hibben's informants said represented constel-
lations of stars.*

fifteenth-century life at Pottery Mound. Additional ingredients in the cultural mix were trade and other connections westward into the upper Little Colorado River and Hopi realms. The resulting infusion of talent and ideas and the stimulation inherent in aggregation may have been relatively short lived, but for a time out on the bleak Puerco a noteworthy response was shown in enigmatic wall paintings.

The Pottery Mound panels provide opportunities for comparative analysis with the two earlier Pueblo IV mural finds. One topic of special interest is the illustrated clothing shown on human and anthropomorphic figures of both sexes. So far as is known, Pueblo peoples of these periods did not tailor clothing but made use of lengths of cloth wrapped in appropriate ways around their bodies. Short lengths held in place by wide sashes became kilts for the men, and longer pieces secured over one shoulder were mid-calf dresses for women. The most common garments were plain black (Fig. 56), but especially at Awatovi and Pottery

Fig. 56. Frontal figure holding parrot in each hand. Colors are black, white, tan, and rust.

Mound black cloth frequently was enriched with white circles or small squares arranged in lines or frets (Fig. 57). Such yardage was depicted in a notable Pottery Mound panel showing three pieces suspended from a frame line across the top of the design field (Fig. 58). Perhaps this was a portrayal not of everyday garb but of material stored in the kiva for ceremonial purposes. Other special clothing indicated in the murals were elaborately painted, embroidered, or tie-dyed shirts and kilts. At Awatovi embroidered bands of small geometrical elements comparable to those on coeval pottery were shown at the ends of sashes and bottoms of kilts. They probably became stylish after Pottery Mound Pueblo was abandoned.

Another interesting textile element in the Puerco paintings is what appears to be cotton blankets hanging from the same frame line as the clothing yardage (Fig. 58). They are shown as large rectangles bearing broad diagonal stripes of maroon, brown, dark green, and purple colors with narrow, horizontal, geometrical borders. Several similar drawings at Awatovi were too fragmentary to give Smith a hint as to their meaning (Fig. 44), but the Pottery Mound murals suggest these Awatovi drawings also might have represented blankets. Their colors differ from those at Pottery Mound and their designs are meanders rather than diagonals.[9] In both cases the base cloth likely was painted. These illustrations have particular significance because thus far no actual blankets of the fifteenth century have ever been found, even though in the early historic period the Hopi were known for their voluminous and fine production of them.

It is probable that cotton of the Hopi type was raised along the Puerco and the weaving of it was an important activity. Hibben noted holes in kiva floors that he regarded as being for anchoring bases of vertical looms.[10] The blanket images may also confirm an active trade in such commodities from Hopi to Pottery Mound and other Eastern Pueblo settlements.

Another wall painting component of note is the female figures. They are more common in the Kuaua and Pottery Mound murals than in those of the Hopi, and many of them represent a sort of generic Pueblo

Fig. 57. Maiden wearing traditional off-the-shoulder, black-and-white blanket dress and conventional buns of hair over the ears. A row of similar figures, shown above the knees, encircled the four walls of Kiva 16. Facial features missing on the original mural were added to the published illustration.

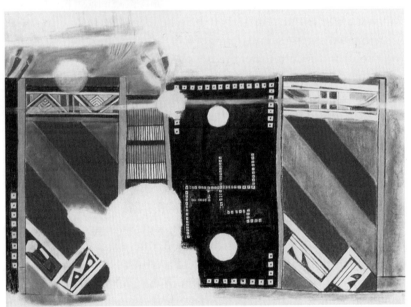

Fig. 58. Suspended textiles. The center black rectangle with linear and circular white patterns was clothing fabric. The rectangles at right and left probably were representations of painted cotton blankets. Repeated textiles of these types occurred around all four walls of one kiva. Colors were gray, brown, black, and white.

woman. Their stocky bodies face forward, they are dressed in the typical off-the-shoulder, short garment, and their arms are bent upward at the elbows. Their hands hold special ritual objects, and their faces, whether painted or partially masked, are expressionless (Figs. 56, 57). They easily could step off the walls and into a present-day line of dancers rhythmically shuffling their way to syncopated drum beats around a regional plaza. Such continuity of custom over at least six centuries may be unnerving to those twentieth-century folks for whom change, often for change itself, is an article of faith. Yet tour buses park bumper to bumper on feast days at the pueblos, bringing their loads of the curious just to witness such linkage with the past.

A further example of tradition everlasting is in the indicated hairdos of these young women. Over their ears are conventionalized black blocks with a sidewise chunk removed on the outer edge (Fig. 57). This device is interpreted as representing buns of hair, which anthropologists studying Pueblo social culture believe is a sign of virginity. Why, where, and when this custom took hold is unknown, but figures with such coiffures appear on sixth-century pottery, in these fifteenth-century paintings, and in photographs of females from the nineteenth and early twentieth centuries. They confirm a lengthy adherence to a single style that would be a modern hairdresser's worst nightmare.

On a more serious note, Patricia Vivian, who undertook interpretation of the symbolism of many of the Pottery Mound wall paintings, suggested that one dominate theme related to the War Society. She saw the colorful panels of a line of male figures holding large decorated shields before them (Fig. 59) as depictions of performers waiting their turn to act in ritual combat during one phase of a Winter Solstice ceremony.[11] Other, similar so-called warriors shown in the murals holding shields, bows and arrows, and quivers may have been engaged in this or other rites rather than in actual fighting. Motifs such as Sun Shields, snakes, bear paws, mountain lions, lightning, and stars probably were understood references to the War Society and its War Gods. They were of utmost importance because they could seek to control weather and the forces of nature.

Fig. 59. Two males carrying ceremonial shields. These figures were part of a frieze of similar figures extending around all four walls of Kiva 2 at Pottery Mound. Colors are rust, tan, black, white, and yellow.

The most striking difference between humans and anthropomorphs in the Puerco wall paintings and those of the Jeddito are in lesser details of costuming. Headdresses, necklaces, shields, and wands appear more frequently in the Puerco paintings (Figs. 59, 60). It is uncertain whether this reflects a stronger outside influence in the central Rio Grande district during the fifteenth century or whether the inhabitants of the Puerco community enjoyed a more prosperous situation than their Antelope Mesa counterparts.

Among secondary background elements of design common on the Pottery Mound murals are birds and feathers. Both were important to the ancient Pueblos for mundane and ritualistic purposes, as they are today. Their frequent depiction in these wall paintings in part must be attributed to the community's proximity of just a long day's walk down the Rio

Fig. 60. Row of three seated figures in profile, serpent and birds overhead, that Hibben terms "Council of Chiefs." Colors are rust, tan, black, white, and yellow.

Puerco into the Rio Grande valley and then to the Bosque del Apache wetlands, where millions of migratory birds now winter and no doubt did so in the past. Enterprising craftsmen could have gathered stockpiles of feathers of many colors and sizes for enhancement of staffs, prayer sticks, shields, headdresses, kilts, and a host of other items. The drawing of a gangly, long-legged crane, Mallard ducks, and other waterfowl verify familiarity with the bird refuge. More important decoratively were parrots and macaws, which had been imported from northern Mexico to the Mimbres region and then on to the northern Southwest since at least the eleventh century. (Fig. 56).[12] Their distinctive physical features and coloration symbolizing directions having particular implied significance and the graceful curves of their feathers made them popular motifs to the

Hopi and Hopi-inspired artisans. Parrots continued to be hallmarks of late historic Acoma pottery.

Probably correctly, the Acomans claim Pottery Mound Pueblo as an ancestral home. With mounting curiosity, occasionally some of them visited the site while excavations were underway. They offered their views on a few figural elements in the murals, and Hibben accepted them uncritically. Whether accurate or not or whether all Acomans agreed on those interpretations, both Anglo and Indian observers were impressed by the artists' skills in draftsmanship, their bold sense of symbolic color, and their imaginative articulation of the abstract. Still, the understory meanings of their imagery, which Brody sees as metaphors of a mystic world,[13] have evaporated like echoes on the wind.

That this is so is evident in the example provided by the all-black, humanlike figures, or isolated balloon heads (Fig. 61). At Kuaua, Dutton's informant called such an element Ka'nashkule, a priest-clown-medicine man. He said another similar personage was a representation of Cha'kwena'okya, ancient woman.[14] Smith suggested that a comparable element at Awatovi recalled a modern Hopi predatory katsina.[15] He did not attempt to identify a second type of black figure. Round black faces without bodies and usually placed against a four-point star stood for the souls of the dead, according to some Acoma visitors.[16] Such heads appear on snake bodies. Patricia Vivian interprets some of the black figures as the War God.[17] Disparity of interpretation may stem from regional distinctions or, more likely, from the impossibility of literally translating metaphors.

Much of the katsina-related painting at Pottery Mound struck Hibben as being inspired by Mexican examples. Indeed, other students of the subject concur, although not necessarily in the identification of specific items with Mesoamerica, but rather in the total package of traits they regard as part and parcel of the katsina cult. Still, some renditions appear to have derived from other backgrounds. For instance, two examples of horned snakes recall the Quetzalcoatl legend. Brew suggested a relationship with the Aztec god Tlaloc but offered no supporting evidence.[18] Other features, such as masked dancers, may have been inspired by

Figure 61. Black figures or black faces that make occasional appearances in all three primary mural sites but are unidentified or interpreted differently. (a) Kuaua: figure identified as Ka'nashkule, priest, clown, or medicine man.

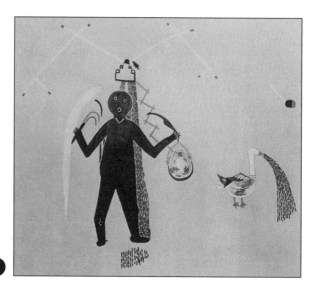

(1)

(2)

(3)

(b) Pottery Mound: (1) rattlesnake with black face called "soul face," perhaps representing spirit of the dead; (2) ghostlike figure descending to earth; (3) unidentified black figure. (c) Awatovi: figure unidentified except to note that facial features are similar to some modern Hopi predatory katsinas.

sources other than those pertaining to katsinas. Certainly the two personages in Figs. 64 and 65[19] wearing exuberant feathered *tablitas*, or headpieces, could easily have lost themselves in a crowd of central Mexican dancers. The way in which figures in profile are drawn seated likewise resembles southern pictorials (Fig. 60). Peoples of southern climes may have been at Pottery Mound in spirit, but to what extent?

From the first American encounters with ruins of the northern Southwest, a Mexican connection was postulated in the erroneous belief that the local Indians were too primitive to have built such sophisticated structures. The well-known Aztec myth of their having come from "the north" further fueled the notion. Scholars soon rejected that idea. Settlers moving west after the Civil War did not. They peppered maps with place-names such as Montezuma, Cortez, and Aztec, and even named the first Arizona territorial capital after William Prescott, a historian who wrote an erudite account of the fall of the Aztec Empire.

As prehistoric studies mounted during the twentieth century, researchers agreed that the fundamental ideas of agriculture and the pottery-making technology had diffused north from higher civilizations in central Mexico. But the question of greater southern impact has for the past sixty years divided the archaeological community into two camps. One camp is made up of those who believe that goods; less tangible aspects of social, economic, or religious nature; and even *pochteca* traders came from the south into the Pueblo world and left their mark. The other camp includes those who think that virtually all cultural evolution in the north was internal. Possibly Hibben leaned toward the first explanation because of being influenced by work going on concurrently at the great center of Casas Grandes in Chihuahua, where a strong central Mexican architectural component was uncovered.

The intellectual promise of the archaeological work at Pottery Mound Pueblo was largely unfulfilled. With hindsight, it is evident that the choice of Pottery Mound as the locale for a field school was a mistake. The ruin was too large and complex to be adequately investigated without far greater commitment than was forthcoming. Nonetheless, from an instructional standpoint the program might be termed successful.

Three students used the recovered information in master of arts theses. Jerry Brody, later professor of art history and director of the Maxwell Museum at the University of New Mexico, and Patricia Vivian, highly successful contemporary artist, wrote about the iconography of the murals. Charles Volk, later in the administrative ranks of the National Park Service, analyzed the pottery. Following that analysis, the bulk of the assortment of studied potsherds was given to the women of Acoma Pueblo to be used as temper for their own fine pottery. It seemed a fitting passing of the torch. A fair number of other participants and graduate student supervisors continued in archaeology or related disciplines. Others learned through experience that this was not for them. That in itself is an important part of education.

However, as far as adding to knowledge about the eras prior to the period of cultural upheaval caused by Spanish colonization, the results of the Pottery Mound project were disappointing. Hibben failed to produce a technical report on the village plan, architecture, or lesser items of material culture of what once must have been a flourishing trade center dominating a wide expanse of the central Rio Grande district. Were special objects comparable to those in the murals recovered from the excavations? Were any identifiable as of Mexican derivation? What was the inventory of ordinary domestic goods? If this location was attractive for the ancestral Pueblos, why was it abandoned? Where might the inhabitants have gone? Instead of considering these and other relevant aspects of the ruin, Hibben focused entirely upon the wall paintings as being more newsworthy. Therein lay some problems.

By the 1950s Frank Hibben was on the way to becoming the most controversial figure in Southwestern archaeology. His personality and lifestyle set him apart. He was charismatic, flamboyant, and, like others with those qualities, given to self-promotion. His passion for hunting large game animals took him around the globe and provided a repertory of stories of his far-flung exploits that captivated audiences. Some tales likely were true; no doubt some were apocryphal. Together they attracted a wide circle of influential admirers outside of the archaeological community. But on the dark side, academic colleagues were privately doubting Hibben's scholarship and his scientific integrity. His most highly publicized and extraordinary finds could not be verified, making some wonder if they too were apocryphal.[20] Department gossip leaked to students. Serious students who had participated in the field school felt uneasy about the carelessness employed in matching the decorative colors and the possible enhancement of some of the figural mural details. These concerns marred an otherwise exciting experience for them.

Twelve years passed before Hibben presented the Pottery Mound wall paintings to the public. With the aid of private monies, he hired a professional artist to render enlivened copies of the field drawings, many of which had been prepared by Patricia Vivian, and to subsidize their publication by a nonacademic press. The end result was a coffee-table-type book with full-page and two-page illustrations printed in brighter than original colors to compensate for presumed fading upon exposure to the brilliant New Mexico summer sunlight. Comparisons between field drawings and those used for publication reveal modifications of minor details. Both procedures are questionable. The accompanying text is weak with incorrect or unsubstantiated statements.

The university now has title to the Pottery Mound ruins. In the late 1970s and early 1980s a field school party, directed by Linda Cordell, salvaged a small house unit there that was threatened by the wash, and a Continuing Education group, led by Hibben, worked in the primary mounds. No additional painted kivas were uncovered.

In 1988, without the obligatory New Mexico State Land Office and Cultural Properties Review Committee permits or approval of the university's oversight board, Hibben and some friends returned to dig in Pottery Mound and a nearby small site situated on state trust lands. An official report was filed accusing him of willful pothunting.[21] The one-time golden boy of New Mexico archaeology had become a discredited rogue.

Portfolios of mural reproductions made from field drawings and a file of colored slides of them and of work in progress are curated at the Maxwell Museum. Hibben retained student excavation notes and drawings ordered for his book.

Regardless of how the Pottery Mound murals may have been mistreated, they stand as a significant contribution to our understanding of Pueblo achievement and thought. It is a pity that they are beclouded by controversy and that the original records are today beyond the reach of further scientific study.

Notes

1. Hibben, 1975, 21.
2. Ibid., 6, 21.
3. Ibid., 6–10.
4. Ibid., 2.
5. Ibid., 4.
6. Ibid., title page, Figs. 47–48; Anne Woolsey, personal communication, May 19, 1998.
7. Hibben, 1975, 10.
8. Ibid., 6.
9. Smith, 1952, Figs. 83a–b, 85a–c, 86c.
10. Hibben, 1975, 20.
11. P. B. Vivian, 1961, 53–74.
12. Creel and McKusick, 1994, 510–524.
13. Brody, 1971; Brody 1991.
14. Dutton, 1962, Figs. 61a, 95.
15. Smith, 1952, Fig. 51b.
16. Hibben, 1975, Figs. 106, 107.
17. P. B. Vivian, 1961, 61–63.
18. Brew, 1944, 241–245.
19. Hibben, 1975, Figs. 64, 65.
20. Preston, 1995, 66–83.
21. Gomolak, 1988.

Salt Flats and Salvation

The archaeological site of Gran Quivira has had more names than a common thug may have aliases. The first Spanish name, Cueloze, probably was a corruption of the term supplied by Tompiro-speaking natives. Its use was discontinued in the seventeenth century for a more familiar linguistic convention, and the place became Pueblo de las Humanas after the name by which the Indians there were known. The name Humanas also appears in documents spelled as Jumanos because the Spanish language was not yet standardized, but the pronunciation was basically the same (although the two spellings reflect a gender difference). In the unfathomable way of folklore, at some time this pile of Indian debris was transformed in the popular mind into what was left of the golden city for which Coronado and his followers searched. The place became commonly known as Gran Quivira. Even those who were blindsided by visions of easy wealth could see that its walls were not golden, but they steadfastly believed there was a treasure trove in its precincts. In 1909 that name was formalized when the ruins of two represented cultures and 611 surrounding acres were proclaimed Gran Quivira National Monument.

In 1980 under the Carter administration the group of structures was re-named Salinas National Monument because at that time the culturally related sites of Abó and Quarai, formerly New Mexico state monuments, were administratively included. Within the past decade has come another change, this time to Salinas Pueblo Missions National Monument. At present some archaeologists have come back to using the Spanish name Las Humanas, while to old-timers the place remains Gran Quivira.

The first Spaniards who ventured into the unknown north country were lured there by dreams of treasure. One place it was to be found was Quivira. From then until now those fantasies remain deeply embedded in the Southwestern ethos. Legends of hidden riches sprout like dandelions in springtime and take fantastic forms. Spanish treasure, lost gold mines, the riches of the Aztec Empire — whatever — it's all out there somewhere waiting to be found.

One version of the Gran Quivira tale had seventy priests at the mission church there when in 1680 the Pueblo Indians rose up in bloody revolt against their Spanish oppressors.[1] (Only one or two priests are documented as having been at Gran Quivira at any time. The town and its church were abandoned at least eight years before the Pueblo Revolt.) Just two priests escaped a massacre within the church. (No human remains ever have been found there.) Apparently alerted to the possible attack, the clergy hastily placed two weighty bells and smaller sacred and precious objects in a deep pit outside the compound. (New Mexico mission churches were extremely poor, with a rare candelabra, humble maiolica vessels for the altar, and worn vestments as their furnishings.) A map giving the location of the buried treasure was carved on a stone sunk into the dirt floor in front of the altar. (And the priests were in a hurry to escape? No such stone has been unearthed.) The surviving priests copied the map on paper and fled, never to be seen again. (*Adios. Vaya con Dios.*)

An even more implausible story is that the Indians, threatened themselves, took their valuables (of which they had none) and those of the priests (who likewise had none) into a natural cavern eaten out of the limestone stratum under the village. An earthquake then rocked the countryside, preventing their escape and leaving them to die with their riches in hand.[2] In an official document published in 1854, the cavern became a stone cellar three hundred yards downhill from the church.[3]

Over the years local Hispanics, a party of Texans, and unknown others plugged the church compound, cemetery, and hillsides beyond to leave gaping holes that resembled an eruption of mud geysers and yielded nothing. No story of this feverish quest was more quixotic than that of the Yrisarri family who, with blind faith, periodically dug there for some 150 years.[4] It seems that in the late eighteenth century the family patriarch acquired a map from an Indian in El Paso that purported to provide the exact location of the Gran Quivira treasure. The question of how an illiterate Indian came to have such a map a century after the town had been abandoned did not deter this man. Even though his pits turned up nothing but dirt and rocks, he willed the map to a son. The son, in turn, willed it to his son, and thus the map went down through the generations until the early years of the twentieth century. By that time someone else in the family had mysteriously found a stone scratched with a diagram indicating where the cache was hidden. Using these references, Jacobo Yrisarri went to work in 1916 or thereabouts and shortly was arrested and fined for digging on public lands without a permit. But he was not to be thwarted in his race for the pot of gold.

During the Great Depression, when men were on the prowl all over the West trying to find a lifesaving bonanza, Alfredo Otero posted a $500 bond and was granted a digging permit that he turned over to the indefatigable Yrisarri. With a little financial backing and a crew of cousins and friends, he began a veritable mining operation right in the middle of Gran Quivira. From the perspective of today's preservation consciousness, it is shocking that the National Park Service would have allowed that to happen, but it was confirmed by none other than Secretary of the Interior Harold Ickes.

The diggers sank a vertical shaft forty feet along a fissure in the limestone stratum, hit solid rock, and then tunneled horizontally another forty feet. A windlass for hoisting the tailings above ground reared over the pit. A government engineer inspected the workings and reported that the shafts were timbered and also that there were caverns honeycomb-ing the limestone. The adit was to break through into an underground passageway leading from the main church to the cellar at the foot of the hill on which the site is situated. Just four feet short of that accomplish-ment, the crew laid down picks and shovels and went home for the 1932 Christmas holidays. While they were gone, the digging permit expired. At that point the National Park Service authorities recognized the error of their ways and refused to renew it.

Without doubt there are those Yrisarris who still believe. This is not to say that there was no treasure at Gran Quivira. It simply did not have monetary value.

The settlement of Gran Quivira was the largest of a string of proto-historic towns scattered along the western skirts of the huge Estancia bol-son east of the Manzano Mountains of central New Mexico. It spread over the crest of a low tableland at the southern end of the basin where sagebrush, saltbush, and sparse stands of dwarf pinyon and juniper now struggle to survive but doubtless were not present during human occu-pation. Without a source of running water and with thin, infertile soil, the site would seem an unlikely location for people dependent to some degree on horticulture. Yet in its heyday Gran Quivira may have housed several thousand individuals within its limestone walls. That is what at-tracted the Franciscans.

The first priest, one Fray Francisco Letrado, arrived at Gran Quivira in 1629.[5] He put the natives to work erecting a small chapel while he, re-putedly, occupied a portion of the pueblo. His tenure was a brief two-and-a-half years, after which he went to Zuni and then to Heaven. Dur-ing the ensuing three decades the people of Gran Quivira dismantled the chapel bit by bit for construction materials to be used elsewhere. Raiding Apaches finished the job in 1652. A second campaign to save the souls of the Gran Quivirans began in 1660 when Padre Diego de Santan-der moved into Letrado's apartment. With an available supply of stone and plentiful labor (by some accounts the women and juveniles of the town), he oversaw the construction of a church and convento planned on a monumental scale. It was so large, in fact, that a dozen years later it remained unfinished.

Meanwhile an excessive burden of tribute in the form of cotton textiles and foodstuffs was demanded by the citizen-soldiers (*encomenderos*) who controlled surrounding rangelands. The most debilitating demand of Spanish overlords was for slabs of hard salt hacked out of deposits in the Estancia lagoons some twenty miles distant, known to the Spaniards as the Salinas province because of this resource (*sal* being the Spanish word for salt). The salt was transported by ox carts guided on foot by these Indians six hundred miles south to Parral, Chihuahua, to be used in the amalgamation process at the silver mines there. The Spaniards made a practice of seizing Apaches, whose traditional territory stretched across southern New Mexico and northern Mexico, to work as slaves in the mines. Expectedly, the Apaches responded fiercely by killing off Spaniards willy-nilly and whatever Native Americans they saw as allies of the enemy. That included the hapless sedentary farmers of the Salinas province. For many preceding years these two Indian groups had been trading partners, salt being one commodity the Quivirans could obtain in abundance. That relationship broke down completely in the mid 1600s. Ultimately continuing Apache raids, combined with deterioration of an already marginal farming environment and uncompromising Spanish demands, ended in desertion of the entire Salinas province during the 1670s. An estimated pre-Spanish population of ten thousand was reduced to zero.[6]

One by one disheartened families at Gran Quivira gathered up a few possessions, strapped their babies onto cradleboards, and walked away, leaving their dead and their bittersweet memories behind. Probably they went down into the Rio Grande corridor to merge with local groups who were suffering the same abuses but not as severely. Together they took revenge in the Pueblo Revolt of 1680. Thereafter the Salinas people lost their identity and their language.

The shell of the roofless San Buenaventura church commanded the west side of a large plaza at Gran Quivira. Its high, thick walls caught the wind and echoed with the folly of zealotry and mindless subjugation. Father Santander moved on.

The proclamation of Gran Quivira as a national monument early in the twentieth century did not mean the arrival of uniformed personnel ready to tidy up the place. For years it remained a quiet, untended chunk of landscape dominated by the ghostly relic of San Buenaventura. Some of its lofty stone walls cascaded down to drift across the nave and the maze of convento walls. Carved wooden lintels loomed as skeletons against the sky. Higher on the mesa slope, emptied dwellings caved into heaps of gray limestone blocks and were covered over with dislodged mortar and windblown earth.

It was not until the 1920s that archaeological attention was given to Gran Quivira. From 1923 through 1925 Hewett, the dynamo at the helm of the School of American Research in Santa Fe, had on the scene a few stalwarts in his growing number of trainees in prehistoric matters. In the party were some whose names would become cornerstones in regional research, such as Odd Halseth (museum director), Lansing Bloom (historian), J. C. Harrington (linguist), Fred Kaboti (Native American artist), Frank Pinkley (National Park Service administrator), and Anna Shepard (ceramic expert).[7] They concentrated on removing the debris from the ecclesiastical buildings. In addition, they undertook cursory digging in a few domestic units, kivas, and burials. As was unfortunately the case with much such exploration prior to World War II, Hewett did not write a report on the work but did include descriptions of the church in a later general book on Spanish missions in the state.[8]

Next came the National Park Service. In response to growing visitation to places of historical interest, officials decided to upgrade exhibits at Gran Quivira by interpreting more of the site for the public. Gordon Vivian was assigned the job. After student apprenticeships under Hewett's supervision at Chaco Canyon and Kuaua, Vivian spent much of his adult life as a National Park Service archaeologist back at Chaco, repairing old structures there and training a crew of local Navajos in the emerging subdiscipline of ruins stabilization. Vivian would load camp and digging gear into the back of a big truck and take off throughout the

Southwest region to carry out such work as was needed in various of the federal installations. The gypsies of the trade, Vivian and his crew in the spring of 1951 came to Gran Quivira, set up camp in the lee of the hillside, and prepared to go to work.

Out of consideration of time and money allotted for excavation and stabilization, Vivian elected to clear the small, L-shaped San Isidro chapel at the lower southern edge of the town plaza and rid it of the unsightly scars left from random searches for buried treasure. Yrisarri's vertical shaft in the apse and sanctuary had destroyed the floor and some walls of the rooms and produced tailings that obscured this part of the building. For safety reasons, National Park Service employees earlier had filled the tunnel opening, but the detritus remained to be hauled off. Considering the wanton destruction, it was amazing that a scatter of plaster scraps showed that Father Letrado's church had been enriched with some sort of wall paintings.[9] Vivian interpreted them as having been a dull red dado banded at the top by a black border above which was a conventionalizd floral pattern in black over a white ground. The fragments were too small for determination of whether or not the upper decoration had been imitations of tiles, as such decorations were at Awatovi. It seemed not to have been the case.

As was customary, the *campo santo* (holy ground, or cemetery) was in front of San Isidro. Vivian expected to find interments there, but they were few in number because of the relatively short usage of the church and limited Christianization of the populace. One puzzling circumstance did come to light when the men dug down along an outer wall in order to repair it. They came upon what appeared to have been the dispersed and incomplete remains of a dozen or more individuals put into a mass gave. They were left in place. Vivian speculated that many more human bones lay beyond his trenches and that possibly these persons had succumbed to a two-year famine known to have ravaged the countryside from 1666 to 1668.[10] Or, the dead may have been victims of Apache assaults. It is not the sort of human tragedy that researchers like to encounter.

Next the men excavated a block of three dozen domestic cells between the chapel and the San Buenaventura convento, on the site map designated as Mound 10. Finally they opened up a circular kiva isolated in the plaza. Unlike what had transpired at Awatovi, the Franciscans assigned to the Salinas province did not put their religious buildings over those of their neophytes. Other clues suggest they may not have been as rigid in their dealings with these Native Americans as some of their brothers in other sectors of New Mexico.

Vivian's Navajo crew was hardworking and competent. Many of them had been a part of the mobile stabilization unit for a number of years and needed little supervision. Others were second generation stabilizers in what was becoming a sort of craft guild, with Vivian as the master. They were thankful for the security of being government employees. This was business as usual for them, not the foolhardy treasure hunting that had gone on here before.

The National Park Service project resulted in a permanent exhibit displaying Native American and European aspects of this particular ruin within confined circuits suitable for the viewing public. It also provided a sampling of the material culture of a people at a critical point in their history. This was fully described in a monograph that Vivian soon prepared.[11]

To a man the crew was relieved to leave Gran Quivira. Incessant winds made work in the open troublesome. The winds seemed to be constant and came from all directions. No matter how shovelers stood, loosened dirt blew up in their faces. When the breezes did die down, plagues of no-see-ums made life more miserable. Now, the men told each other, they knew the real reasons why the ancients had pulled up stakes and left, and it was not because of their Athabascan relatives, the Apaches.

As Vivian said farewell to Jack Kite, the caretaker, he asked him to call collect if the wind ever stopped. Years later Kite greeted the next contingent of excavators with the news that he had never had to make that call to Vivian. He did not smile as he said it.

Wind and all, for three seasons from 1965 through 1968 Gran Quivira was subjected anew to archaeological scrutiny. This time the goal was to excavate the primary ruin complex, Mound 7, the largest of nineteen

Fig. 62. Alden Hayes, left, consulting with crew members Jerry
Green and Gary Fulger, Gran Quivira, 1967.

other houses on the crest and slopes of the mesa. Alden Hayes, veteran
National Park Service archaeologist, was put in charge for what was to be
his major solo show. He, too, was a product of Hewett's 1930s embrace of
New Mexico prehistory but had been sidetracked by military service and
an abortive fling at ranching, only to come back to the archaeological
fold in the late 1950s. By this time the romanticized allure of adventure
had vanished. The Hayes operation was all business. He hired laborers
from nearby Mountainair, primarily ranchers down on their luck. Totally
without academic pomposity, using a colorful cowboy lingo, and sharing a deep love of the land, Hayes quickly established a comfortable rap-
port with them (Fig. 62). Certainly he did not need to instruct them in
how to use shovels, trowels, and wheelbarrows, as had been the work of
Hibben's assistants at the student digs at Pottery Mound.

This 1960s crew commuted to work over a paved road and at quitting
time went home. The first season Hayes lived in a small stone house at

the site, later to become the Visitor Center, and thereafter occupied a commodious house trailer complete with flush plumbing, gas stove, electric lights, and refrigerator. Gone were the good old days when the archaeologist slept on the ground without air mattress, ate cold chili out of a can, drank cowboy coffee boiled to double strength over a fire, bathed in a tin wash basin, and wondered when he could get to the nearest post office to learn whether his sweetheart was still his. In his heart, Hayes, being Hayes, would have preferred it that way.

Day by day the hired hands, with Hayes at their sides, dug up the secrets long hidden beneath the earthy shroud of Mound 7. They had been rendered confused and complicated by four hundred years of continuous occupation on this spot. Contrary to expectations, there was no multistoried edifice there. Instead the high mound had been created by five successive building episodes, one on top of another, with layers of fill and refuse in between.[12]

To build one's house over refuse was not as offensive as it might seem. Trash then was not what trash is now. These people did not have metal, glass, plastics, rubber, or paper. Theirs was not a throw-away society but one that used everything to the nth degree. What was left to be discarded was little more than a few worn stone implements, broken crockery, and hearth sweepings of ash and bits of charcoal. There were no food scraps other than animal bones and corn cobs. Things made of plant fibers — such as basketry, sandals, aprons, or cordage — or wooden objects seldom survived in sites in the open air. Therefore, what the archaeologist typically had to work with actually was a mere fraction of the hardware of everyday life. But it did accumulate and generally got tossed into the nearest empty room or surface depression. As portions of the settlements fell into decay, they became depositories and often were stripped of usable stones and timbers. Thus filling up and tearing down went on simultaneously until, if new constructions were desired, it was easiest to level off these piles and build on top rather than move to virgin ground. Besides, home was where it always had been.

The settlement being lived in when the Spaniards arrived was a warren of more than two hundred contiguous, small cells that were one story in height.[13] Numerous tree-ring dates place its construction in the second half of the sixteenth century. The houseblock took on a vague F-shaped configuration. Five subterranean, circular kivas of Eastern Pueblo style were beyond the houseblock. All construction was of irregularly shaped blocks of limestone laid up in mortar made of surface dirt and fine trash. Hewett, ever the romantic, thought the bluish gray coloration of the buildings imparted a spectral feeling, in sharp contrast to the resolute stability conveyed by the deep red sandstone used at Abó.[14] Such characteristics would have been of little consequence, since presumably all surfaces were mud-plastered. Entry into core rooms was by means of hatchways in the ceilings. Without light or fresh air, living in these units must have been unpleasant and unhealthy. Most daytime activities surely took place outdoors. Mealing bins on rooftops, perhaps once sheltered by *ramadas* or windbreaks, confirm this.

Indian garden plots of corn, beans, squash, cotton, and a few invading nondomesticates lay around the base of the ridge. The priests' gardens likely were among them, but no evidence of introduced European vegetables or fruits was found — nor was any search made for them. Sand dunes on the south side of the slopes afforded some protective mulch. The gardens were dependent upon natural precipitation, of which there either was too little or too much — in the form of gullywashers. Surveys of the region did locate more than thirty shallow wells, which could have been used for pot irrigation when the rains did not come at all. More commonly, they provided domestic water. The many large, flat-backed, earthenware canteens the diggers recovered were used to carry water from the wells to the hearths. Additionally, Hayes and his team found eight adobe-lined pits dug into bedrock within or near the houses; Hayes speculated that these may have been cisterns to capture runoff from the slopes or rooftops.[15]

Colonial records indicate that when Father Letrado assumed his conversion tasks at Gran Quivira, he preempted some rooms of the pueblo, but just which ones are not specified. Hayes was able to locate them precisely because of architectural modifications. Some of these were in an eight-room cluster of the Mound 7 structure nearest to where the apse of

Fig. 63. Father Letrado's convento and apartment in Mound 7; plaza with unfinished San Buenaventura church and convento in background.

Letrado's chapel was going to be.[16] They would serve as a ready-made convento. Assuming that an Indian family occupied two rooms, that meant he displaced four families. Subsequently, as a personal apartment, Letrado had native builders add eight much larger rooms wrapped around the outside of those old rooms (Fig. 63). Their walls were up to three feet thick and were plastered on the interior, and there was one beveled window. Had he come from rural Mexico or Spain, Letrado would have felt comfortable in these crude stone-and-mud structures because they were not too unlike those he would have known before. Nevertheless, he needed privacy and so had the original connecting openings into the Indian structure sealed. He wanted wider doorways with splayed jambs and lower sills than were typical of Indian houses. He saw that the two doorways opening into the plaza had heavy pine doors, both of which the diggers found.[17] Obviously they had been fashioned with metal tools.

To ward off winter's chill that settled into stone masonry rooms, he had a corner fireplace erected in one room. An iron pot hook anchored in one wall implied that the room might have been used for cooking. The other rooms presumably were for sleeping, reading, praying, and storage. No latrine was identified.

Father Letrado's quarters were extravagant when compared with those of his next-door neighbors. He probably felt he deserved them as a reward for having to do God's work in this harsh land where the whirling wind never abated.

The clerical establishment must have been furnished with an altar, benches, tables, washstand, shelves, and bedstead made of rough pine. Excavators found none of those items. Because of the Apache threat, the province lay empty for much of the eighteenth century, but when Spanish settlers again braved this frontier and prospectors came in search of treasure, it is suspected that they scavenged whatever such things remained scattered about.

The two padres were in residence at Gran Quivira for a combined fifteen years. The amount of rubbish left by this brief, poverty-stricken tenure would have been minimal. Excavations turned up just a few scraps that Hayes could identify as definitely Spanish. Some heavily corroded metal tools such as a hoe, three hatchets, knife blades, nails, and fragments of uncertain usage were part of the kit of work implements allotted to each mission. Several pieces of glass came from jars or flasks. One hopes that an exotic wheel-turned sherd might have been part of a jar of olive oil or sacramental wine that added a bit of pleasure to a solitary life in the hinterland. Most significant in terms of their global history were very small sherds of tin-glazed maiolica ceramics and one piece of Chinese porcelain.

Hayes's later report does not specifically describe the maiolica, but other research shows that two types of maiolica plates or jars were sent from central Mexico to seventeenth-century outposts in New Mexico and northern Arizona. One had blue decorations on a creamy white ground. The other bore brilliant designs in yellow, orange, green, blue, and brown on white. Researchers named this latter type Abó Polychrome after several nearly complete vessels that they found at the Salinas Abó mission in the early 1940s and described as a distinct class.[18] This was an unfortunate choice of names because the pottery was made in Puebla, Mexico, some fifteen hundred miles away. Nonetheless, a few handleless cups and saucers of this and its companion style got included in the supply caravans moving north every three years.[19]

The historical background of maiolica pottery goes back to wares that were made in the eighth-century Muslim caliphates in what is now Iraq and then spread across North Africa and into Spain. Spanish artisans settling in Mexico in the sixteenth century brought their technology with them and produced maiolica wares of different styles, according to their backgrounds in the motherland. Abó Polychrome, dated generally to the second half of the seventeenth century, was Italianate in its colors and designs. That added another dimension to the story of this pottery. Its distinctiveness from anything the Pueblo Indians had ever seen must have made a big impression, even though the number of vessels in the colony was small. The floral motifs on the San Isidro walls might well have been inspired by this ware.

One can scarcely imagine a more amazing record than that associated with the one tiny splinter of porcelain removed from the dirt at Gran Quivira.[20] It was from an object made half way around the world in a porcelain factory town in central China. Millions of vessels of several grades were manufactured there, then nested in chests or crates and sent by river barges down to Hong Kong. There the ceramics were loaded onto junks to cross the South China Sea to Manila. In due time the crates were stacked in the hold of a Spanish galleon making an annual three-month voyage up past the Japanese islands, across the north Pacific, and down the west coast of North America to Acapulco. Squads of *cargadores* carted the cargo of precious Oriental goods, including the porcelain, up to the highlands and Mexico City. The great volume of low-grade Chinese porcelain coming into Mexico made it so inexpensive that it was sent out by civil and church authorities to all reaches of the Spanish colonial empire. One distribution route by creaking ox-drawn carts was up the *meseta central* of Mexico to far-off Santa Fe. After all this jostling around in a half dozen different kinds of conveyances over thousands of miles of rough seas and rougher trails, an intact, eggshell-thin, glassy rice bowl, tea cup, or saucer survived to be used on Father Letrado's or Father Santander's altar or table — that was almost miraculous.

As a daily routine the priests ate and drank from the same earthenwares as were used by the Quivirans. However, it was only natural for the padres to want some things more in keeping with their own lifeways. A few ceramic finds point up the poignancy of their feelings of being cut off from familiar surroundings. The native potters customarily turned out hemispherical bowls of varied sizes to be used communally by a dining group. That kind of sharing likewise had been commonplace in medieval Spain. But seventeenth-century Europeans were more sophisticated in their preference for individual serving dishes. And, of course, the priests ate alone. Very likely they gave sketches to potters of what they remembered as common porringers, or soup bowls, and requested that one or more be made for them. Such vessel form was suitable for the stews that were the priest's usual fare. The result of the potters' efforts was a plain grapefruit-size bowl, mounted on a thick coil of clay intended to duplicate the ring foot of a wheel-turned vessel, with a horizontal flaring rim of exaggerated width.[21] While serviceable, the vessel was of ludicrous proportions and bore only slight resemblance to Spanish tableware. Moreover, being unglazed, the bowls assuredly made any hot foodstuffs served in them taste like mud. We hope the good Fathers were tolerant, for how were the women to know?

The priests also ordered some squat, stable, clay candleholders.[22] Unlike the Indians, the priests were not accustomed either to sitting in the dark or to retiring at nightfall. Wax candles, the manufacture of which was a household craft introduced to the northlands by the Spaniards, must have been a source of amazement to the natives. They previously had enjoyed night illumination only by torches or in the glow of firepits.

With the short life spans that prevailed at the time, and with the human presence at Gran Quivira lasting for four centuries, deaths there must have numbered into the many hundreds. Because Pueblo peoples customarily left their dead in graves within or near their settlements,

Hayes and his workers expected to find some of them. The excavations did produce the physical remains of more than 550 individuals.[23] Undoubtedly many more lay in the warmth of unexcavated or inaccessible places. It was not entirely unexpected that in the late stages of occupation of Gran Quivira, cremation was practiced by some while flexed inhumations were carried out by others. A similar situation had been found earlier at a neighboring small village.

These were the two places in the northern Southwest where researchers noted this duality of burial practices. Cremations were not a Pueblo custom. However, they did occur at Zuni, presumably as a result of influence from farther south. From the clear evidence of the burning of human bodies discovered at Mound 7 and the simultaneous introduction there of a different style of pottery, Hayes postulated that a contingent of peoples from Zuni or the Cibola province in the west fled eastward after the fierce battles at Hawikuh when Coronado and his entourage arrived in 1540.[24] Further support for this probable influx of refugees was that they may have settled in outer Mound 7 rooms believed to post-date 1545.

The Catholic Church did not sanction cremation. It must be assumed that if these acts were carried out during times when the Franciscans were at the Gran Quivira settlement, they were done in secret. That may explain why a high percentage of the burial pits for cremated persons were under the floors of occupied rooms. Father Letrado would have been outraged had he known that after his departure two burial pits for calcined bones were sunk into the dirt floor of one of the rooms of his convento. Was this defiance, or what?

Exhuming burials is not a ghoulish pastime for archaeologists. Nor is any disrespect for the dead intended. It is a lamentable fact that former cavalier excavation and curation methods gave the impression that human skeletons were considered mere artifacts. Too often the remains were not studied but were simply stored in museum cabinets to collect dust. In fairness, it should also be noted that once the spirit of a dead person drifted off to join the natural spirits of the universe, the Indians themselves often demonstrated disregard for human bones. All that aside, the circumstances of death and the ways in which this inevitable part of the human experience are treated provide unmatched opportunities for insight into past events that may not be otherwise recognized and into mental attitudes generally not accessible to those who deal primarily in material things.

One example of a story-behind-the-story came when the excavation crew at Gran Quivira reconstructed a dramatic scene that involved neither method for disposal of the dead. In Kiva N, which at some time had suffered obvious fire damage, they exposed skeletons of two individuals.[25] One was that of a woman in her late twenties and the other was a youth about sixteen years old. Both were sprawled on the kiva floor face down in heaps of partially burned roofing materials. Near the bodies were several unshaped slabs of limestone. In Hayes's scenario of events here, these unfortunates were victims of a raid and had fallen through a collapsing, burning roof and probably died of smoke inhalation. The stone slabs may have been missiles thrown in on top of them. Their relatives left the bodies where they fell, gradually to be buried under eight feet of trash. This one revealed bit of the past speaks volumes about violence, suffering, and resignation.

Regardless of mode of death, all retrieved skeletal materials were studied and reported by Erik K. Reed, National Park Service archaeologist, and Christy Turner, professor at Arizona State University.[26] As far as the archaeological community was concerned, it not only was acceptable but expected that burials would be photographed and analyzed. Nowadays were such remains encountered, they would be left in place or reburied according to the dictates of whomever could prove former affiliation. The Native American Graves Protection and Repatriation Act (NAGPRA) legislation passed in the early 1990s placed restrictions on this aspect of archaeological inquiry.

Those who chose to settle at this location had migrated northward out of Jornada Mogollon territory about the 1300s. Slowly they were influenced by ancestral Pueblos dwelling along the Rio Grande valley to the west. Pithouses and surface wattle-and-daub structures of Mogollon derivation gave way to surface masonry buildings of adjoining rooms and subterranean ceremonial chambers having attributes comparable to those of the Pueblos. Gradually and unknowingly, Quivirans were transformed into being Pueblos. Still, whether it was the drag of their more humble beginnings or whether it was because they dwelt in the perceived boondocks, they always seemed a step or two behind their more with-it Pueblo associates.

An example of this cultural lag is apparent in the wall paintings excavators detected soon after work commenced in the most recent levels. Three kivas and seven rooms retained evidence of such imagery. In all instances, the decorated plaster was extremely fragmented and, to use a Smith phrase, in a condition of "advanced decrepitude."[27] Prehistorically, the walls of the kivas had been reinforced with vertical poles over which thick coats of mud had been spread in order to hold them in place and to provide a smooth surface. Plaster laid on top in some cases was brown adobe but more commonly was a mix of wood ash and sand that dried to a light gray color. All the kivas had been razed in the past, their upper limits removed or vandalized, and their interiors later partially filled with trash. This process eliminated much of the upper portions of the murals but helped protect from two to four feet of the lower surfaces. The paintings on room walls had suffered similarly.

Barbara Peckham, National Park Service employee in the Gran Quivira laboratory in Santa Fe and experienced in dealing with the Pottery Mound murals, came to the site to record these finds.[28] She experienced the frustrations of tracing crumbling, incomplete panels as she worked from the surface inward and agreed with Hayes that there was little that could be salvaged.

There were two exceptions in Room 12. One was a five-foot-long, narrow panel just a foot-and-a-half above the floor. It showed a line of multicolored, elongated human figures, no more than sixteen inches tall, who appeared to be dancing (Fig. 64). One figure had a black stripe down his middle that might be interpreted as the kind of body painting reported

Fig. 64. Late-phase walls in Room 12, Mound 7, painted with polychromatic, dancing human figures and two horizontal rows of white dots.

for these people. It recalls a Kuaua figure identified as a white Salimo-piya.[29] Others were adorned with what must have been intended as flowing feather accessories. To attempt the removal and preservation of this and another abstract body of design so that Peckham could study them in a horizontal position to prevent their further scaling, Hayes sought the help of Gordon Vivian.[30] Vivian had not undertaken this kind of work since his school days thirty years before at Kuaua but remembered the methods used there. For a week he and Hayes, working under a temporary roof, spread rolls of wet yellow toilet paper over the plaster units and

Fig. 65. Temporary protective covering during removal of thirty-one plaster layers in Kiva N, Mound 7; remains of Franciscan church and convento in background.

then covered them with burlap strips soaked in liquid plaster-of-paris (Fig. 65). They removed one vertical course of the rock masonry behind the prehistoric plaster and extended the new jacket down the back side of the panel one row of masonry at a time. Finally, when the encased wall sections were standing free, they bolted them with two-by-fours that were then covered with plaster strips (Figs. 66, 67). These jacketed murals were taken to Santa Fe for stripping and analysis, where they were cut apart with a surgical saw.

The paintings that could be discerned were totally unlike coeval ones from any of the prehistoric sites to the west. Making use of a more restricted palette of colors, the Quivirans executed illustrations that fell into three vague types. Most common were small geometrics, especially

Fig. 66. Workers preparing materials for jacketing painted wall fragments, Mound 7, 1967.

Fig. 67. Jacketed wall fragments with wall paintings, Mound 7.

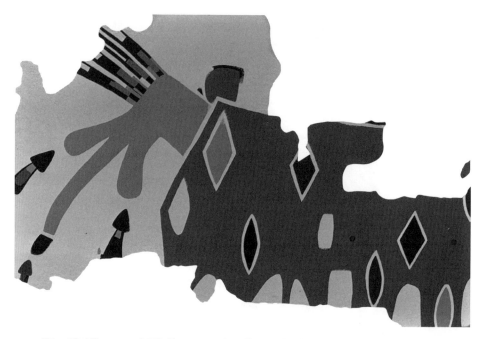

Fig. 68. The most skillfully executed wall panels of polychromatic geometric elements recovered at Mound 7.

round white dots in horizontal rows. Squares, rectangles, and irregular shapes were outlines or filled motifs such as solid bands of color (Fig. 68). Other panels resembled regional pictographs but were placed on interior wall surfaces (Fig. 69). Most of these were white elements on black or brown grounds. Humans or anthropomorphs were small in scale and generally abstract. The details of dress or trimmings on the humans were merely suggestive or nonexistent. Fields of design were unstructured. Most works were of inept or uninspired draftsmanship. The sizes of the remaining examples were so tiny, or were only borders of what must have been more elaborate depictions, that they are almost unintelligible, and judgments about their significance must be tentative.[31]

Researchers assumed these wall paintings were somehow part of katsina rites. Perhaps their judgments were biased by the Pueblo example.

Fig. 69. Small white quadruped, plant, and dot elements on black band just slightly more than a foot above floor of Kiva N. This is a middle-phase construction with obvious relationship to regional pictographs. The wall surfaces were damaged by fire.

However, that interpretation may not be totally correct. One representation seems to be a round-faced mask, but actually there is little else resembling katsina imagery as rendered elsewhere. The dancing figures in Room 12 could have been engaged in some other kind of ritual. Moreover, aside from the mainly unintelligible pieces of depictions, there was no enclosed plaza at Gran Quivira nor any rectangular kivas such as were universal in other places where the katsina ceremonies were enacted. Nevertheless, elements that do recall katsina masks appear on the local pottery, indicating some familiarity with the cult repertory. It may be that these people either were not so dedicated to the cult as their fellows to the west or they lacked the artistic sensibilities or skills to display its icons in more typically Pueblo ways. Maybe this was provincialism at work.

Whatever the religious implications, wall painting was practiced at Gran Quivira for at least 250 years. Kiva N, scene of the violent deaths of two individuals, produced the largest number of painted panels, twenty-four in all out of thirty-one plaster layers. Judging from eight structural timbers, the chamber was erected in 1416, but the archaeologist had no way of knowing exactly when it was no longer used or when each of the painting efforts was made. Later rooms were put over this kiva and its trashy contents, leading Hayes to assign it to his middle phase of site occupation. Late-phase Room 12, whose erection occurred about a century and a quarter later, also had been plastered thirty-one times with twenty-three decorated layers. But, interestingly enough, such decorative treatment in this room may have been carried out during just a dozen years before everyone moved away. If such a concerted effort did occur, it may have been because of Father Santander.

The saving of souls and oversight of them to prevent backsliding had been lax at Gran Quivira. Letrado's short stint there followed by almost thirty years of only occasional visits by the priest from Abó allowed the residents to continue their traditional practices without significant interference. When Santander took up his mission in 1660, he came with instructions to stamp out such paganism. The Hayes crew found that all five Gran Quivira kivas had been destroyed, an action they attributed to Santander's zeal. Whereupon, in Hayes's opinion, the unrepentants converted at least seven inner sanctum cells in their houseblock, where the priest was not apt to have the temerity to intrude, into kivas complete with walls that were painted periodically as required by prescribed rituals.[32] If Santander realized he had been outdone, he apparently made no attempt to demolish those units. Time alone took care of that.

Today an attractive new Visitor Center in a style harmonious with the setting has replaced the 1930s dingy stone house in which archaeologist Hayes once camped. Specimens recovered in his dig and that of Vivian are displayed attractively. In a colorful reproduction, the line of figures from the fifteenth layer of Room 12 dance along one wall. Those are the treasures of Gran Quivira.

Notes

1. Works Progress Administration, 1940, 399.
2. Hewett and Fisher, 1943, 165.
3. G. Vivian, 1964, 31.
4. Ibid., 31–33, for detailed account of the Yrisarri treasure hunting at Gran Quivira.
5. Hayes, 1981, 7, 31; G. Vivian, 1964, 22.
6. Hayes, 1981, 8.
7. Ibid., V.
8. Hewett and Fisher, 1943, 165.
9. G. Vivian, 1964, 78–79.
10. Ibid., 80.
11. G. Vivian, 1964.
12. Hayes, 1981, 15.
13. Ibid., 16, Map 5.
14. Hewett and Fisher, 1943, 165–166.
15. Hayes, 1981, 20–22, 24–25.
16. Ibid., 31, Fig. 21.
17. Ibid., 34–35, Figs. 29–31.
18. Lister and Lister, 1987, Fig. 144c.
19. Hurt, 1990, 185, Photos 17–18, and 167–168, Pls. 23–24; Toulouse, 1949, 40, Pls. 25–28.
20. Lister and Lister, 1976, 113–140; Lister and Lister, 1987, 234–235.
21. Hayes, 1981, 62, Fig. 105.
22. Ibid., 161, Fig. 214.
23. Ibid., 169.
24. Ibid., 176.
25. Ibid., 53.
26. Reed, 1981, 75–118; Turner, 1981, 119–122.
27. Smith, 1972, 8.
28. Peckham, 1981, 15–38.
29. Dutton, 1962, 171, Fig. 11.
30. Hayes, personal communication, February 3, 1998.
31. Hayes, 1981, 52–53, Figs. 74–75; Peckham, 1981, 19, Fig. 21.
32. Hayes, 1981, 61.

References

Adams, E. Charles

1991   *The Origin and Development of the Pueblo Katsina Cult.* University of Arizona Press, Tucson.

Adams, Jenny L.

1994   *Pinto Beans and Prehistoric Pots: The Legacy of Al and Alice Lancaster.* Arizona State Museum, Archaeological Series no. 183. Tucson.

Anderson, Frank G.

1955   The Pueblo Kachina Cult: A Historical Reconstruction. *Southwest Journal of Anthropology* 11, no. 4: 404–420.

Bliss, Wesley L.

1936   Problems of the Kuaua Mural Paintings. *El Palacio* 40, nos. 16–18: 81–86.

1948   Preservation of the Kuaua Mural Paintings. *American Antiquity* 13, no. 3: 218–222.

Breternitz, David A.

1966   *An Appraisal of Tree-Ring Dated Pottery in the Southwest.* University of Arizona, Anthropology Papers no. 10. Tucson.

Brew, John Otis

1937 The First Two Seasons at Awatovi. *American Antiquity* 3, no. 2: 122–137.
1944 On the P IV and on the Katchina-Tlaloc Relations. In *El Norte de México y el Sur de Estados Unidos*. Tercera Reunión de Mesa Redonda sobre Problemas Antropológicos de México y Centro América, pp. 241–245. Mexico, D.F.
1949a The History of Awatovi. In *Franciscan Awatovi*, by Montgomery, Smith, and Brew. Papers of the Peabody Museum of American Archaeology and Ethnology, vol. 36, pt. I, 2–43. Cambridge, Mass.
1949b The Excavation of Franciscan Awatovi. In *Franciscan Awatovi*, by Montgomery, Smith, and Brew. Papers of the Peabody Museum of American Archaeology and Ethnology, vol. 36, pt. II, 47–108. Cambridge, Mass.
1952 Foreword. In *Kiva Mural Decorations at Awatovi and Kawaika-a*, by Watson Smith. Papers of the Peabody Museum of Archaeology and Ethnology, vol. 37, vii–xii. Cambridge, Mass.

Brody, J. J.

1971 *Indian Painters and White Patrons*. University of New Mexico Press, Albuquerque.
1991 *Anasazi and Pueblo Paintings*. School of American Research Press, Santa Fe.

Creel, Darrell, and Charmion McKusick

1994 Prehistoric Macaws and Parrots in the Mimbres Area, New Mexico. *American Antiquity* 59, no. 3: 510–524.

Crotty, Helen K.

1992 Protohistoric Anasazi Kiva Murals. *Papers of the Archaeological Society of New Mexico* no. 18: 51–62. Albuquerque.
1995 Anasazi Mural Art of the Pueblo IV Period AD 1300–1600: Influence, Selective Adaptation, and Cultural Diversity in the Prehistoric Southwest. Ph.D. dissertation, University of California at Los Angeles.

Dutton, Bertha P.

1962   *Sun Father's Way: The Kiva Murals of Kuaua.* Museum of New Mexico, School of American Research, and University of New Mexico Press, Albuquerque.

Elliott, Melinda

1995   *Great Excavations.* School of American Research Press, Santa Fe.

Gomolak, Andrew R.

1988   Investigation of Unauthorized Excavation in the Hidden Mountain Area, NW 1/4 of 36, T7N, R2W, NMPM, Valencia County, N.M. Report of Commissioner of Public Lands, State of New Mexico, Santa Fe.

Hack, John T.

1942a   *The Changing Physical Environment of the Hopi Indians of Arizona.* Papers of the Peabody Museum of American Archaeology and Ethnology, vol. 35, no. 1. Cambridge, Mass.

1942b   *Prehistoric Coal Mining in the Jeddito Valley, Arizona.* Papers of the Peabody Museum of American Archaeology and Ethnology, vol. 35, no. 2. Cambridge, Mass.

Hale, Gardner

1966   *The Technique of Fresco Painting.* Dover, New York.

Hayes, Alden C.

1981   *Excavation of Mound 7, Gran Quivira National Monument.* National Park Service, Publications in Archeology no. 16. Government Printing Office, Washington.

Hewett, Edgar Lee

1938   The Frescoes of Kuaua. *El Palacio* 45, nos. 6–8: 21–29.

Hewett, Edgar Lee, and Reginald G. Fisher

1943   *Mission Monuments of New Mexico.* University of New Mexico Press, Albuquerque.

Hibben, Frank C.

1955   Excavations at Pottery Mound, New Mexico. *American Antiquity* 21, no. 2: 179–180.
1960   Prehistoric Paintings at Pottery Mound. *Archaeology* 13, no. 4: 267–275.
1966   A Possible Pyramidal Structure and Other Mexican Influences at Pottery Mound, New Mexico. *American Antiquity* 31, no. 4: 522–529.
1967   Mexican Features of Mural Paintings at Pottery Mound, New Mexico. *Archaeology* 20, no. 2: 84–87.
1975   *Kiva Art of the Anasazi.* KC Publications, Las Vegas.

Hough, Walter

1903   Archeological Field Work in Northwestern Arizona: The Museum-Gates Expedition of 1901. In *Report of the U.S. National Museum for 1901*, 279–358. Government Printing Office, Washington.

Hurt, Wesley R.

1990   *The 1939–1940 Excavation Project at Quarai Pueblo and Mission Buildings, Salinas Pueblo Missions National Monument, New Mexico.* National Park Service, Southwest Cultural Resources Center, Professional Paper no. 29. Santa Fe.

Kent, Kate Peck

1957   *The Cultivation and Weaving of Cotton in the Prehistoric Southwestern United States.* American Philosophical Society, Transactions, vol. 47, pt. 3. Philadelphia.
1983   *Pueblo Indian Textiles: A Living Tradition.* School of American Research Press, Santa Fe.

Lister, Florence C., and Robert H. Lister

1976   Distribution of Mexican Maiolica Along the Northern Borderlands. *Papers of the Archaeological Society of New Mexico* no. 3, 113–140. Albuquerque.

1987 *Andalusian Ceramics in Spain and New Spain.* University of Arizona Press, Tucson.

Luhrs, Dorothy L., and Albert G. Ely

1939 Burial Customs at Kuaua. *El Palacio* 46, no. 2: 27–32.

Martin, Paul S.

1936 *Lowry Ruin in Southwestern Colorado.* Field Museum of Natural History, Anthropology Series, vol. 23, no. 1. Chicago.

1937 Early Development in Mogollon Research. In *Archaeological Researches in Retrospect,* edited by Gordon R. Willey, 3–32. Winthrop, Cambridge, Mass.

Montgomery, Ross Gordon

1949 San Bernardo de Aguatubi, An Analytical Restoration. In *Franciscan Awatovi,* by Montgomery, Smith, and Brew. Papers of the Peabody Museum of American Archaeology and Ethnology, vol. 36, pt. III, 112–288. Cambridge, Mass.

Montgomery, Ross Gordon, Watson Smith, and J. O. Brew

1949 *Franciscan Awatovi: The Excavation and Conjectural Reconstruction of a 17th-Century Spanish Mission Establishment at a Hopi Indian Town in Northeastern Arizona.* Papers of the Peabody Museum of American Archaeology and Ethnology, vol. 36. Cambridge, Mass.

Peckham, Barbara A.

1981 Pueblo IV Murals at Mound 7. In *Contributions to Gran Quivira Archeology, Gran Quivira National Monument, New Mexico.* National Park Service, Publications in Archeology no. 17, 15–38. Government Printing Office, Washington.

Preston, Douglas

1995 The Mystery of Sandia Cave. *The New Yorker,* June, 66–83.

Reed, Erik K.

1981 Human Skeletal Material from the Gran Quivira District. In *Contributions to Gran Quivira Archeology, Gran Quivira National Monu-*

ment, New Mexico. National Park Service, Publications in Archeology no. 17, 75–118. Government Printing Office, Washington.

Schaafsma, Polly, and Curtis F. Schaafsma

1974 Evidence for the Origins of the Pueblo Katchina Cult as Suggested by Southwestern Rock Art. *American Antiquity* 39, no. 4, pt. 1: 535–545.

Smith, Watson

1949 Mural Decorations of San Bernardo de Aguatubi. In *Franciscan Awatovi*, by Montgomery, Smith, and Brew. Papers of the Peabody Museum of American Archaeology and Ethnology, vol. 36, pt. IV, 291–339. Cambridge, Mass.

1952 *Kiva Mural Decorations at Awatovi and Kawaika-a, with a Survey of Other Wall Paintings in the Pueblo Southwest.* Papers of the Peabody Museum of American Archaeology and Ethnology, vol. 37. Cambridge, Mass.

1972 *Prehistoric Kivas of Antelope Mesa, Northeastern Arizona.* Papers of the Peabody Museum of American Archaeology and Ethnology, vol. 39, no. 1. Cambridge, Mass.

1980 Mural Decorations from Ancient Hopi Kivas. In *Hopi Kachina: Spirit of Life*, edited by Dorothy Washburn, 129–138. California Academy of Science, San Francisco.

1992 One Man's Archaeology. *The Kiva* 57, no. 2: 101–190.

n.d. One Man's Archaeology. Typescript, labeled 7th printing. In the possession of Florence C. Lister.

Stout, George L., and Rutherford J. Gettens

1932 *Transport des Fresques Orientales sur de Nouveaux Supports*, 3–8. Mouselon, Paris.

Tichy, Marjorie Ferguson

1938 The Kivas of Paako and Kuaua. *New Mexico Anthropologist* 2, nos. 4–5: 71–79.

1939 The Archaeology of Puaray. *El Palacio* 46, no. 7: 145–163.

Toulouse, Joseph H., Jr.

1949 *The Mission of San Gregorio de Abó: A Report on the Excavation and*

Repair of a 17th Century New Mexico Mission. School of American Research, Monograph no. 13. Albuquerque.

Trimble, Stephen

1993   *The People: Indians of the American Southwest*. School of American Research Press, Santa Fe.

Turner, Christy G.

1981   The ASU Study of Gran Quivira Physical Anthropology. In *Contributions to Gran Quivira Archeology, Gran Quivira National Monument, New Mexico*. National Park Service, Publications in Archeology no. 17, 118–122. Government Printing Office, Washington.

Vivian, Gordon

1935   The Murals at Kuaua. *El Palacio* 38, nos. 21–23: 113–119. Santa Fe.
1964   *Gran Quivira: Excavations in a 17th Century Jumano Pueblo*. National Park Service, Archeological Research Series no. 8. Government Printing Office, Washington. Reprinted 1979, Southwest Parks and Monuments Association, Tucson.

Vivian, Patricia Bryan

1961   Kachina: The Study of Pueblo Animism and Anthropomorphism within the Ceremonial Wall Painting of Pottery Mound, and the Jeddito. Master's thesis, State University of Iowa, Ames.

White, Adrian S., and David A. Breternitz

1976   *Stabilization of Lowry Ruins*. Bureau of Land Management, Cultural Resources Series no. 1. Denver.

Works Progress Administration

1940   *New Mexico: A Guide to a Colorful State*. Workers of the Writer's Program. Coronado Cuarto Centennial Commission, Hastings House, New York.

Archives

Anasazi Heritage Center, Dolores, Colorado.
Center of Southwest Studies, Fort Lewis College, Durango, Colorado.

Crow Canyon Archaeological Center, Cortez, Colorado.
The Field Museum, Chicago, Illinois.
Laboratory of Anthropology, Museum of Indian Arts and Culture, Santa Fe, New Mexico.
Maxwell Museum, University of New Mexico, Albuquerque.
Mesa Verde Research Center, Dove Creek, Colorado.
Museum of Northern Arizona, Flagstaff.

Sources of Illustrations

Alden C. Hayes collection: figs. 62–69.

Anasazi Heritage Center, Dolores, Colorado: fig. 8.

Carol Harrison collection: fig. 25.

The Field Museum, Chicago, Photo Archives: fig. 1 (Neg. No. A925690), fig. 2 (Neg. No. A78653), fig. 3 (Neg. No. A78647), fig. 4 (Neg. No. A78649).

Fort Lewis College, Center of Southwest Studies, Lancaster collection. Durango: figs. 31–36, 46.

Laboratory of Anthropology/Museum of Indian Arts and Culture, Santa Fe. Kuana Series: fig. 11 (Archives No. 1531.7), fig. 15 (Archives No. 1531.17), fig. 61a (No. 131). Kuaua murals: fig. 16 (No. 002, Layer A-8), fig. 21 (No. 109A), fig. 22 (No. 110A), fig. 24 (No. 128, Layer M-40), fig. 26 (No. 025, Layer D-14), fig. 27 (No. 057, Layer H-31), fig. 28 (No. 101, Layer A-8).

Mesa Verde Research Center, Dove Creek, Colorado: figs. 5–7, 9.

Museum of Northern Arizona, Flagstaff. Photo Archives: fig. 29 (NA820.1), fig. 30 (NA820.2), fig. 37 (NA820.10), fig. 38 (NA820.10M), fig. 39 (NA820, R229.1), fig. 40 (NA820, R3: 3A), fig. 41 (NA820, R529.6), fig. 42 (NA820, R2.1), fig. 43 (NA820, R3.23), fig. 44 (NA820, R3.19B), fig. 45 (NA1001, R2.2), fig. 61c (NA820.51b).

R. Gwinn Vivian collection: figs. 12–14, 17–20, 47, 49–52.

Robert H. Lister collection: frontispiece, fig. 10, 23.

University of New Mexico Maxwell Museum. Photo Archives: figs. 48, fig. 53 (76.70.586), fig. 54 (76.70.205), fig. 55 (76.70.650), fig. 56 (76.70.648), fig. 57 (76.70.589), fig. 58 (76.70.585), fig. 59 (76.70.205), fig. 60 (76.70.635), fig. 61b (76.70.205, 76.70.208, 76.70.314).

Index